THE SIN
THE ULTIMAT

MW01489836

LAS VEGAS

TRAVEL GUIDE

DIANA L.
MITCHELL

Dear reader, thanks a lot for purchasing my book.

To help you plan your trip even more efficiently, I have included an interactive map powered by Google My Maps.

To access it, scan the QR code below.

Happy travelling!

A Note to Our Valued Readers

Thank you for choosing this travel guide as your companion for exploring the world.

I want to take a moment to address a concern you might have regarding the absence of photographs in this book.

As an independent author and publisher, I strive to deliver high-quality, informative content at an affordable price.

Including photographs in a printed book, however, presents significant challenges. Licensing high-quality images can be extremely costly, and unfortunately, I have no control over the print quality of images within the book.

Because these guides are printed and shipped by Amazon, I am unable to review the final print quality before they reach your hands.

So, rather than risk compromising your reading experience with subpar visuals, I've chosen to focus on providing detailed, insightful content that will help you make the most of your travels.

While this guide may not contain photos, it's packed with valuable information, insider tips, and recommendations to ensure you have an enriching and memorable journey.

Additionally, there's an interactive map powered by Google My Maps—an essential tool to help you plan your trip.

I encourage you to supplement your reading with online resources where you can find up-to-date images and visuals of the destinations covered in this guide.

I hope you find this book a helpful and inspiring resource as you embark on your next adventure.

Thank you for your understanding and support.

Safe travels,

Diana

Table of Contents

Welcome to Las Vegas

Welcome to Las Vegas, a dazzling oasis in the desert known as the "Sin City". Bursting with energy and excitement, Las Vegas is a playground of glitz, glamour, and endless possibilities, making it one of the most dynamic cities in the world. Whether you're a first-time visitor or a seasoned traveler, the city's iconic skyline, vibrant nightlife, and unparalleled attractions offer endless opportunities for adventure and indulgence.

Las Vegas is composed of a variety of distinct areas—The Strip, Downtown Las Vegas, Summerlin, and Henderson—each with its unique character and charm. From the world-famous resorts and casinos of The Strip to the historic allure of Downtown, the upscale neighborhoods of Summerlin, and the serene communities of Henderson, there's something for everyone in Las Vegas.

The city is home to some of the world's most famous landmarks, such as the Bellagio Fountains, the Welcome to Fabulous Las Vegas sign, and the Stratosphere Tower. It's a global hub for entertainment, boasting world-class shows, concerts, and nightlife. Whether you're exploring themed casinos, catching a Cirque du Soleil performance, strolling through luxury shopping centers, or savoring culinary delights from around the globe, Las Vegas promises an unforgettable experience.

Join us as we guide you through the best of what Las Vegas has to offer, providing tips and insights to help you make the most of your visit to this extraordinary city.

Why Visit Las Vegas?

Las Vegas is a destination like no other, offering a unique blend of entertainment, luxury, and excitement that captivates millions of visitors each year. Here are some compelling reasons why Las Vegas should be at the top of your travel list:

Iconic Landmarks

Las Vegas is home to some of the world's most recognizable landmarks. From the dazzling Bellagio Fountains, with their choreographed water shows, to the breathtaking views from the High Roller observation wheel and the iconic Las Vegas Strip, these sights are must-sees for any visitor.

Entertainment Extravaganza

Theater lovers and thrill-seekers flock to Las Vegas for its vibrant entertainment scene. With an array of shows, from world-famous Cirque du Soleil performances to magic shows and headliner concerts, there's always something spectacular to see. The city's casinos offer not only gambling but also a variety of live entertainment options.

Culinary Delights

Las Vegas's food scene is legendary, offering everything from Michelin-starred fine dining to iconic buffets. Indulge in gourmet dishes crafted by celebrity chefs, savor international cuisines in upscale restaurants, or explore food markets and street vendors for a true culinary adventure.

Shopping Paradise

Las Vegas is a shopper's paradise, featuring luxury boutiques in The Forum Shops at Caesars, trendy shops at Fashion Show Mall, and unique finds in local markets. Whether you're looking for high-end fashion, vintage treasures, or quirky souvenirs, the city has it all.

Nightlife and Clubs

The nightlife in Las Vegas is unrivaled, with its array of nightclubs, bars, and lounges. Dance the night away at world-renowned clubs like Omnia and XS, enjoy rooftop cocktails with panoramic views, or unwind in stylish lounges.

Natural Beauty and Recreation

Beyond the neon lights, Las Vegas boasts beautiful natural attractions. Red Rock Canyon offers stunning hiking trails and rock climbing opportunities, while Lake Mead provides a serene escape for boating and fishing. The nearby Hoover Dam is a marvel of engineering and offers fascinating tours.

Historical Significance

With its rich history, Las Vegas offers numerous sites of historical importance. Explore the Mob Museum to learn about the city's notorious past, visit the Neon Museum to see iconic vintage signs, and tour the historic Fremont Street for a glimpse into old Las Vegas.

Vibrant Neighborhoods

Each Las Vegas neighborhood has its distinct character and charm. From the artistic vibes of the Arts District and the upscale allure of Summerlin to the historic streets of Downtown, there's always a new area to discover.

Year-Round Attractions

No matter the season, Las Vegas offers a plethora of activities and events. Enjoy pool parties in the summer, festive holiday displays in the winter, springtime festivals, and fall culinary events.

Las Vegas's dynamic spirit, luxurious experiences, and endless entertainment options make it an unforgettable destination for travelers from around the world. Whether you're here for a weekend or an extended stay, Las Vegas promises experiences that will leave you wanting to return time and again.

Getting Around

Public Transportation

Las Vegas has a growing public transportation system that makes it easy to navigate the city without a car. Here's an overview of the key public transportation options, including the bus routes, the Las Vegas Monorail, and the Deuce on the Strip.

Bus Routes

Overview:
- Las Vegas' bus system is operated by the Regional Transportation Commission of Southern Nevada (RTC), providing comprehensive coverage across the city and surrounding areas.
- Buses operate throughout the Las Vegas Valley, with numerous routes connecting key destinations, including the Strip, downtown, and residential neighborhoods.

Types of Buses:
- **Local Buses:** Make frequent stops, serving specific neighborhoods and routes.
- **Express Buses:** Provide faster service with fewer stops, catering primarily to commuters traveling between the suburbs and the city center.
- **Deuce on the Strip:** A popular double-decker bus route that runs along Las Vegas Boulevard, connecting major hotels, casinos, and attractions.

Using the Bus:
- **Fares:** Payment can be made using the RTC's fare payment system. You can purchase passes at ticket vending machines, online, or via the rideRTC app.
- **Bus Stops:** Look for blue and white signs with route numbers. Check schedules and maps posted at stops or use transit apps for real-time information.

- **Boarding:** Enter through the front door and exit through the rear door. Have your fare ready when boarding.

Popular Routes:
- **Deuce on the Strip:** Runs along Las Vegas Boulevard, providing easy access to major hotels, casinos, and attractions from the Fremont Street Experience to the south end of the Strip.
- **SDX (Strip & Downtown Express):** Offers limited-stop service between downtown Las Vegas and the Strip, providing faster travel.
- **Route 109:** Connects McCarran International Airport to the South Strip Transfer Terminal and downtown Las Vegas.

Las Vegas Monorail

Overview:
- The Las Vegas Monorail is a convenient and efficient way to travel along the Las Vegas Strip, with stops at key hotels and attractions.
- Operates seven days a week, with frequent service throughout the day and night.

Monorail Stations:
- **MGM Grand Station:** Southernmost station, connecting to the MGM Grand Hotel and Casino.
- **Bally's/Paris Las Vegas Station:** Access to Bally's and Paris Las Vegas.
- **Flamingo/Caesars Palace Station:** Serves the Flamingo and Caesars Palace.
- **Harrah's/The LINQ Station:** Connects to Harrah's and The LINQ.
- **Las Vegas Convention Center Station:** Ideal for convention attendees.
- **Westgate Station:** Near the Westgate Las Vegas Resort & Casino.
- **SLS Station:** Northernmost station, serving the SLS Las Vegas Hotel & Casino.

Using the Monorail:

- **Fares:** Tickets can be purchased at station vending machines or online. Various pass options are available, including single ride, day passes, and multi-day passes.
- **Accessibility:** All stations and trains are fully accessible for passengers with disabilities.

Public Transportation Tips

Plan Ahead:

Research bus and monorail schedules and routes in advance, especially if you're attending an event or visiting popular areas.

Use Apps:

Download the rideRTC app for real-time updates, route planning, and fare payment.

Stay Informed:

Check for service alerts and updates, particularly during major events and holidays.

Las Vegas' public transportation system provides a range of options to suit your travel needs, whether you're exploring the Strip, heading downtown, or venturing into residential neighborhoods. By utilizing the bus system, the Las Vegas Monorail, and the Deuce on the Strip, you can navigate the city efficiently and enjoyably.

Taxis and Rideshares

Las Vegas offers a variety of taxi and rideshare options that provide convenient and flexible transportation throughout the city. Here's a detailed look at traditional taxis, Uber, and Lyft, including how to use them, fare information, and tips for a smooth ride.

Overview:

- Traditional taxis are a common sight in Las Vegas and are regulated by the Nevada Taxicab Authority.
- They can be hailed on the street, found at taxi stands, or booked through dispatch services.

How to Hail a Taxi:

- **Street Hailing:** Stand on the curb and raise your arm when you see an available taxi. Available taxis will have their roof light illuminated.
- **Taxi Stands:** Commonly located near major hotels, casinos, and transportation hubs like McCarran International Airport.
- **Telephone Dispatch:** You can also call for a taxi through dispatch services provided by various taxi companies.

Fare Information:

- **Base Fare:** Starts at $3.50, with additional charges based on distance and time.
- **Surcharges:** There is a $2.00 airport surcharge for trips originating from McCarran International Airport.
- **Tolls:** Any applicable tolls are added to the fare.
- **Tips:** A customary tip for taxi drivers is 15-20% of the total fare.
- **Payment:** Accepted in cash and credit/debit cards. All taxis are equipped with card readers.

Tips for a Smooth Ride:

- **Provide Clear Directions:** Have your destination address ready and communicate it clearly to the driver.
- **Safety:** Make sure the taxi's license number and driver's information are displayed on the dashboard.
- **Receipt:** Always ask for a receipt at the end of your ride for record-keeping or in case you need to retrieve lost items.

Overview:

- Uber and Lyft are popular rideshare services in Las Vegas, offering convenient, app-based transportation options.
- These services provide a range of vehicle types, from budget-friendly rides to luxury options.

Using Uber and Lyft:

- **Download the App:** Available on both iOS and Android platforms.
- **Create an Account:** Sign up with your email, phone number, and payment information.
- **Request a Ride:** Enter your destination and choose the type of ride (e.g., UberX, UberPOOL, Lyft, Lyft XL).
- **Track Your Ride:** The app provides real-time tracking of your driver's location and estimated arrival time.
- **Payment:** Automatically charged to your registered payment method. Tips can be added through the app.

Fare Information:

- **Base Fare:** Varies by service type and time of day.
- **Surge Pricing:** During peak times or high demand, prices may increase due to surge pricing.
- **Tolls:** Any applicable tolls are added to the fare.
- **Tips:** Tipping is optional but appreciated and can be done through the app.

Service Options:

- **UberX/Lyft:** Standard ride for up to four passengers.
- **UberPOOL/Lyft Shared:** Shared rides with other passengers heading in the same direction, offering a lower fare.
- **UberXL/Lyft XL:** Larger vehicles for groups up to six passengers.
- **Uber Black/Lyft Lux:** Premium black car service for a more luxurious ride experience.

Tips for a Smooth Ride:

- **Confirm Your Ride:** Verify the driver's name, vehicle make, model, and license plate before getting in.

- **Safety Features:** Both apps offer safety features such as sharing your trip status with friends and family and in-app emergency assistance.
- **Pickup Locations:** Choose a safe and convenient pickup location, especially in busy areas.
- **Ratings:** Rate your driver after the ride to provide feedback on your experience.

Comparisons and Considerations

Availability:

- Taxis are typically more abundant around the Strip and downtown areas, while rideshare services can be more convenient in residential neighborhoods or less busy areas.

Cost:

- Rideshare fares can be more variable due to surge pricing, whereas taxi fares are more consistent but may include surcharges during peak times or from the airport.

Convenience:

- Rideshare apps offer the convenience of cashless payment and real-time tracking, while taxis can be easily hailed on the street without the need for an app.

Whether you choose a traditional taxi or a modern rideshare service like Uber or Lyft, Las Vegas provides a range of options to suit your transportation needs. Understanding how to use these services effectively can help you navigate the city with ease and make the most of your time in Las Vegas.

Biking

RTC Bike Share Program

Overview:

- The RTC Bike Share program is Las Vegas' bike-sharing system, offering a convenient and eco-friendly way to get around the city.
- Launched in 2016, it has grown to include numerous bikes and stations primarily in downtown Las Vegas and surrounding areas.

How RTC Bike Share Works:

- **Membership Options:** Choose from various membership plans, including Single Ride, Day Pass, and Annual Membership.
  - **Single Ride:** Best for occasional users, allows a 30-minute ride for a fixed fee.
  - **Day Pass:** Ideal for tourists, offers unlimited 30-minute rides in a 24-hour period.
  - **Annual Membership:** Best for residents, includes unlimited 60-minute rides for a year.
- **Finding a Bike:** Use the RTC Bike Share app or website to locate nearby stations and check bike availability.
- **Unlocking a Bike:** Use the app, your RTC Bike Share key (for annual members), or a ride code to unlock a bike at any station.
- **Riding and Returning:** Enjoy your ride and return the bike to any RTC Bike Share station. Make sure the bike is securely docked to end your ride.

Benefits of Using RTC Bike Share:

- **Flexibility:** Easily navigate through traffic and access areas not well-served by public transportation.
- **Health and Fitness:** Enjoy a workout while commuting or sightseeing.
- **Environmentally Friendly:** Reduce your carbon footprint by opting for a bike over a car or taxi.

Tips for a Smooth Ride:

- **Plan Your Route:** Use the RTC Bike Share app to plan safe and efficient routes.

- **Follow Traffic Rules:** Obey all traffic signals and signs, use bike lanes where available, and signal your turns.
- **Safety Gear:** Always wear a helmet and consider using reflective clothing or lights, especially at night.
- **Station Availability:** Check the app for docking station availability near your destination to avoid last-minute hassles.

Popular Routes and Destinations:

- **The Arts District:** Explore the vibrant and creative heart of downtown Las Vegas.
- **Fremont Street Experience:** Enjoy the bustling pedestrian mall and its attractions.
- **Symphony Park:** Visit this cultural center and its nearby museums and entertainment venues.
- **Las Vegas North Premium Outlets:** Ride to one of the premier shopping destinations for some retail therapy.

The RTC Bike Share program provides an excellent alternative to traditional transportation methods, making it easier to explore Las Vegas while promoting health and sustainability. Whether you're a resident or a visitor, the bike share program offers a flexible and enjoyable way to experience the city.

What to See and Do

Iconic Landmarks

The Strip

The Las Vegas Strip, often simply referred to as "The Strip," is a 4.2-mile-long section of Las Vegas Boulevard known for its concentration of resort hotels and casinos. It is a major destination for visitors from around the world, offering an array of entertainment options, dining experiences, and shopping opportunities. The Strip is not just a place for gambling; it is a comprehensive entertainment district that features everything from world-renowned shows to luxurious spas.

The development of The Strip began in the 1940s with the opening of the El Rancho Vegas, and since then, it has grown into one of the most iconic destinations in the world. The Strip is home to some of the largest and most lavish hotels and casinos, including the Bellagio, Caesars Palace, The Venetian, and MGM Grand. These establishments offer a variety of attractions, such as themed performances, impressive architecture, and opulent interiors.

One of the unique aspects of The Strip is its pedestrian-friendly nature. Visitors can stroll along wide sidewalks and easily access a plethora of attractions. The Strip is also known for its vibrant nightlife, with numerous nightclubs, bars, and lounges offering entertainment into the early hours. Additionally, the area hosts several high-profile events throughout the year, including major boxing matches, concerts, and conventions.

Dining on The Strip is an experience in itself, with an extensive range of culinary options available. From high-end restaurants helmed by celebrity chefs to casual eateries, there is something to suit every taste and budget. Shopping enthusiasts will find a variety of retail options, including luxury boutiques and expansive malls like The Forum Shops at Caesars and The Shops at Crystals.

Overall, The Strip embodies the essence of Las Vegas, blending glitz, glamour, and excitement. It is a must-visit destination for anyone looking to experience the unique energy and attractions that make Las Vegas a world-renowned entertainment hub.

Welcome to Fabulous Las Vegas Sign

The "Welcome to Fabulous Las Vegas" sign is one of the most iconic symbols of Las Vegas. Located at the southern end of The Strip, just beyond the Mandalay Bay Resort, this historic landmark has been greeting visitors since 1959. Designed by Betty Willis, the sign is an enduring piece of Americana and a popular photo spot for tourists.

The sign's design is a testament to the mid-20th century era in which it was created, reflecting the bold and flashy style of Las Vegas. It features a diamond-shaped panel with the words "Welcome to Fabulous Las Vegas Nevada" in bright lights, framed by a border of neon bulbs. The back of the sign reads "Drive Carefully Come Back Soon," a warm farewell to departing visitors.

Betty Willis created the sign as a freelancer, and she deliberately chose not to trademark it, allowing it to become a public domain symbol of the city. Its retro charm and cultural significance have made it a must-see attraction for anyone visiting Las Vegas.

The "Welcome to Fabulous Las Vegas" sign is accessible via a small parking lot, making it convenient for tourists to stop and take photos. It is particularly popular at night when the neon lights are illuminated, creating a quintessential Las Vegas photo opportunity. The sign is also located near several major hotels and casinos, adding to its accessibility for visitors exploring The Strip.

In recent years, the area around the sign has been improved to enhance the visitor experience. A dedicated pedestrian plaza was added, providing a safer and more convenient space for tourists to take photos without disrupting traffic.

The sign represents the glitz, glamour, and excitement that Las Vegas is known for. Whether you are a first-time visitor or a seasoned traveler, a photo with the "Welcome to Fabulous Las Vegas" sign is a classic way to commemorate your trip to this vibrant city.

Bellagio Fountains

The Bellagio Fountains are one of the most iconic attractions on the Las Vegas Strip, offering a mesmerizing display of water, music, and light. Located in front of the Bellagio Hotel and Casino, these fountains have been captivating visitors since their debut in 1998. The fountains are set in an 8.5-acre lake and feature a choreographed water show that combines precision and artistry.

The design and construction of the Bellagio Fountains were undertaken by WET Design, a California-based company renowned for creating water features around the world. The fountains consist of more than 1,200 nozzles that shoot water up to 460 feet into the air, synchronized with a variety of music genres ranging from classical and opera to pop and Broadway hits. The shows are enhanced by over 4,500 lights, creating a stunning visual spectacle.

The Bellagio Fountain shows run every 30 minutes during the day and every 15 minutes in the evening, providing ample opportunities for visitors to catch a performance. Each show is unique, featuring different songs and choreographies, ensuring that no two experiences are the same. Some of the popular songs featured in the fountain shows include "Time to Say Goodbye" by Andrea Bocelli and Sarah Brightman, "Viva Las Vegas" by Elvis Presley, and "My Heart Will Go On" by Celine Dion.

Watching the Bellagio Fountains is a quintessential Las Vegas experience, attracting millions of visitors each year. The best viewing spots are from the sidewalk along Las Vegas Boulevard or from the balconies of nearby restaurants and bars. For a more intimate experience, guests can watch the fountains from the Bellagio's own viewing areas or from rooms and suites that overlook the lake.

The Bellagio Fountains are not just a visual delight; they also represent the grandeur and extravagance that Las Vegas is famous for. Their elegance and precision reflect the high standards of entertainment in the city, making them a must-see attraction for anyone visiting Las Vegas.

Fremont Street Experience

The Fremont Street Experience is a vibrant and iconic destination in downtown Las Vegas, offering a lively blend of entertainment, history, and dazzling visuals. Stretching five blocks along Fremont Street, this pedestrian mall is known for its electric atmosphere, free live performances, and the mesmerizing Viva Vision light show.

One of the main attractions of the Fremont Street Experience is the Viva Vision canopy, which is the largest video screen in the world. Spanning 1,500 feet in length and 90 feet in width, the canopy features over 12 million LED lights and 550,000 watts of sound. Every night, the Viva Vision light shows dazzle visitors with high-definition graphics and synchronized music, creating an immersive and unforgettable experience. The shows run every hour, and themes range from rock concerts to tributes to iconic musicians.

Fremont Street is also home to a variety of street performers, live bands, and entertainers, making it a hub of activity both day and night. The outdoor stages host free concerts featuring local and international artists, adding to the vibrant and festive atmosphere. Visitors can enjoy performances ranging from classic rock and country to jazz and pop.

The Fremont Street Experience is steeped in history, with many of its establishments being part of Las Vegas' early days. Iconic casinos like the Golden Nugget and Binion's Gambling Hall offer a glimpse into the city's storied past while providing modern gaming and entertainment options. The area also features an array of dining options, from classic diners and steakhouses to contemporary eateries and food trucks.

For thrill-seekers, the SlotZilla zip line offers a unique way to experience Fremont Street. Riders can choose between the lower Zip-Zilla line, which runs halfway down the pedestrian mall, and the upper Super-Hero Zoom line, which spans the entire length of the Fremont Street Experience, providing a bird's-eye view of the vibrant scene below.

The Fremont Street Experience encapsulates the spirit of Las Vegas with its blend of old-school charm and modern attractions. It is a must-visit destination for anyone looking to experience the energy, entertainment, and history of downtown Las Vegas.

Hoover Dam (nearby)

The Hoover Dam, located approximately 30 miles southeast of Las Vegas on the border between Nevada and Arizona, is a marvel of modern engineering and a major tourist attraction. Completed in 1935 during the Great Depression, this monumental structure was an unprecedented feat at the time and remains one of the most impressive dams in the world.

Standing 726 feet tall and stretching 1,244 feet across the Black Canyon of the Colorado River, the Hoover Dam was built to control flooding, provide irrigation water, and generate hydroelectric power. The dam impounds Lake Mead, the largest reservoir in the United States by volume when full. The construction of the dam created thousands of jobs and played a crucial role in the economic development of the American Southwest.

Visitors to the Hoover Dam can explore the site through a variety of tours and exhibits. The Hoover Dam Visitor Center offers educational displays and films about the dam's history, construction, and impact on the region. Guided tours provide an in-depth look at the dam's inner workings, including access to the power plant and passageways within the dam. The tours highlight the engineering innovations and human efforts that made the construction possible.

One of the most striking features of the Hoover Dam is the Art Deco design, evident in the elegant details and statues that adorn the structure. The Winged Figures of the Republic, two large statues by sculptor Oskar J.W. Hansen, are particularly noteworthy, symbolizing the dam's significance and the human spirit's triumph over adversity.

The dam's location provides stunning views of the surrounding landscape, including Lake Mead and the Colorado River. The Mike O'Callaghan-Pat Tillman Memorial Bridge, which spans the canyon just downstream of the dam, offers a vantage point for panoramic photographs of the dam and the river below.

The Hoover Dam is not only an engineering wonder but also a testament to American ingenuity and determination. It continues to serve its original purposes of flood control, water storage, and power generation, while also attracting millions of visitors each year who come to marvel at its grandeur and learn about its historical significance. Whether you are a history buff, an engineering enthusiast, or simply a traveler seeking breathtaking views, a visit to the Hoover Dam is an essential part of any trip to the Las Vegas area.

Red Rock Canyon National Conservation Area

Red Rock Canyon National Conservation Area, located just 17 miles west of the Las Vegas Strip, is a stunning natural escape offering a stark contrast to the city's bustling atmosphere. Managed by the Bureau of Land Management, Red Rock Canyon encompasses nearly 200,000 acres of protected land known for its vibrant red sandstone formations, unique geological features, and diverse ecosystems.

The conservation area is famous for its towering red cliffs, which are part of the Keystone Thrust Fault, a significant geological feature that dates back millions of years. These striking rock formations, combined with the area's lush desert vegetation and abundant wildlife, create a breathtaking landscape that attracts over two million visitors annually.

One of the most popular activities at Red Rock Canyon is hiking. The area boasts over 30 miles of hiking trails that cater to all skill levels, from easy walks like the Calico Tanks Trail to more challenging hikes like the Turtlehead Peak Trail. These trails offer hikers the opportunity to explore canyons, ridges, and desert landscapes while enjoying panoramic views of the surrounding area.

For those who prefer a scenic drive, the 13-mile Scenic Loop Road provides a leisurely way to experience Red Rock Canyon's beauty. The loop offers numerous pullouts and viewpoints where visitors can stop to take photos, enjoy the scenery, and access trailheads for further exploration.

Rock climbing is another popular activity in Red Rock Canyon, with climbers from around the world coming to tackle its challenging routes. The area features a variety of climbing options, from beginner-friendly routes to advanced multi-pitch climbs.

In addition to outdoor recreation, Red Rock Canyon is home to a visitor center that provides educational exhibits about the area's geology, wildlife, and cultural history. The center also offers guided tours and ranger-led programs that enhance visitors' understanding and appreciation of this unique natural environment.

Red Rock Canyon National Conservation Area is a haven for outdoor enthusiasts and nature lovers. Its stunning landscapes, recreational opportunities, and proximity to Las Vegas make it an essential destination for anyone looking to experience the natural beauty of the Mojave Desert.

Seven Magic Mountains

Seven Magic Mountains is a striking art installation located in the desert just south of Las Vegas. Created by Swiss artist Ugo Rondinone, this large-scale public artwork features seven towering stacks of brightly colored boulders, each standing between 30 and 35 feet high. The installation has become an iconic destination, drawing art enthusiasts, photographers, and tourists alike since its unveiling in May 2016.

The project was produced by the Art Production Fund and the Nevada Museum of Art, with the intention of creating a unique visual experience that contrasts with the natural desert landscape. The vibrant colors of the painted boulders stand out dramatically against the muted tones of the surrounding environment, creating a surreal and captivating visual effect.

Seven Magic Mountains is located approximately 10 miles south of the Las Vegas Strip, near Jean Dry Lake, and is easily accessible by car. The installation's location in the vast desert landscape emphasizes the contrast between human creativity and the natural world, inviting viewers to contemplate the intersection of art and nature.

Visitors to Seven Magic Mountains can explore the site freely, walking around the towering rock formations and taking in the impressive scale of the artwork. The installation is especially popular for photography, with the colorful boulders providing a stunning backdrop for creative and artistic shots. The play of light and shadow on the rocks throughout the day adds to the dynamic visual experience, making it a captivating subject for both amateur and professional photographers.

The installation was originally intended to be a temporary exhibit, with a planned duration of two years. However, due to its immense popularity and cultural significance, efforts have been made to extend its presence, allowing more visitors to experience this unique and thought-provoking artwork.

Seven Magic Mountains has become a symbol of the vibrant and eclectic art scene in the Las Vegas area. Its bold colors and dramatic setting offer a memorable and visually striking experience, making it a must-visit destination for anyone traveling to southern Nevada.

AREA15

AREA15 is a cutting-edge entertainment and art complex located just minutes from the Las Vegas Strip, offering a fusion of immersive experiences, art installations, retail spaces, and live events. Opened in 2020, AREA15 is a one-of-a-kind destination that blends the lines between art, technology, and entertainment, making it a must-visit spot for both locals and tourists seeking something beyond the typical Vegas experience.

One of the standout attractions within AREA15 is Meow Wolf's Omega Mart, a surreal, interactive art installation that masquerades as a grocery store but quickly transforms into a mind-bending journey through otherworldly landscapes and hidden passageways. Omega Mart invites visitors to explore its bizarre environments, uncover secret narratives, and engage with the art in a highly personal and interactive way. It's an experience that challenges perceptions and encourages exploration, creativity, and curiosity.

In addition to Omega Mart, AREA15 features a variety of other immersive attractions. Museum Fiasco is a space that uses lights and sounds to create an intense sensory experience, while Wink World by Blue Man Group co-founder Chris Wink offers a psychedelic take on infinity mirror rooms, combining lights, color, music, and humor. The LIFTOFF ride gives visitors a bird's-eye view of the Las Vegas skyline, offering a new perspective on the city.

Beyond the attractions, AREA15 hosts an array of events, from live music performances and DJ sets to art exhibitions and themed parties. The venue's diverse offerings make it a dynamic space that's always evolving, ensuring there's something new and exciting every time you visit.

The complex also includes a variety of dining and shopping options, with a focus on the eclectic and the extraordinary. From unique food trucks to immersive bars like Oddwood, which features a glowing tree centerpiece, AREA15 offers a full sensory experience that goes beyond mere consumption.

Overall, AREA15 is more than just a destination; it's a reimagined world where art, entertainment, and technology converge to create an unforgettable experience. Whether you're looking to explore the avant-garde, experience a new type of nightlife, or simply see something completely out of the ordinary, AREA15 is a place where the extraordinary becomes the norm.

Neon Boneyard

The Neon Boneyard, part of the Neon Museum in Las Vegas, is an outdoor exhibit that offers a unique glimpse into the city's storied past through its iconic neon signage. Situated just a short distance from the bustling Strip, the Neon Boneyard is home to more than 200 unrestored signs, each telling a story of Las Vegas's vibrant history and its evolution into the entertainment capital of the world.

The signs at the Neon Boneyard come from some of the most famous casinos, hotels, and businesses in Las Vegas history, many of which no longer exist. Walking through the Boneyard feels like stepping back in time, with signs from the Stardust, the Riviera, and the Moulin Rouge, among many others. These signs, once the beacons that lit up the Las Vegas skyline, now serve as historical artifacts that reflect the changing tastes, styles, and fortunes of the city.

Guided tours are available and highly recommended, as they provide rich context and stories behind the signs. Knowledgeable guides share insights about the design and technology of neon signs, the cultural significance of these glowing icons, and the role they played in defining Las Vegas's unique aesthetic. They also highlight the restoration efforts that preserve these pieces of history for future generations.

The Boneyard is not just about nostalgia; it's also a celebration of the artistry and craftsmanship that goes into neon sign design. The collection showcases different styles and eras of neon, from the elaborate designs of the mid-20th century to the more minimalist trends of the later decades. At night, select signs are illuminated, offering a stunning visual experience that captures the magic of old Las Vegas.

In addition to the main Boneyard, the Neon Museum offers other exhibits, including the North Gallery, which features additional signs and a light show called "Brilliant!" This show uses projection mapping to bring the old signs to life, recreating their original glow in a visually stunning display.

The Neon Boneyard is a must-visit for anyone interested in the history of Las Vegas, design, or Americana. It's a place where the city's past is preserved and celebrated, offering visitors a deeper understanding of the evolution of one of the world's most iconic cities.

Gold & Silver Pawn Shop

The Gold & Silver Pawn Shop is one of the most famous pawn shops in the world, largely due to its starring role in the popular television series "Pawn Stars." Located on Las Vegas Boulevard, a short distance from the Fremont Street Experience, this shop has become a major tourist attraction in its own right, drawing fans of the show and those interested in unique collectibles.

Founded in 1989 by Richard "Old Man" Harrison, the Gold & Silver Pawn Shop is a family-run business that quickly rose to fame after "Pawn Stars" premiered on the History Channel in 2009. The show, which follows the daily operations of the shop and the interactions between the Harrison family and their customers, became a massive hit, turning the shop into a must-see destination for visitors to Las Vegas.

The shop itself is a treasure trove of rare and unusual items, ranging from historical artifacts and vintage toys to luxury watches and fine art. Visitors can browse the displays to see a variety of items, many of which have been featured on the show. Some of the shop's most famous pieces include rare coins, autographed sports memorabilia, and even a Super Bowl ring.

What makes the Gold & Silver Pawn Shop stand out is not just the eclectic mix of items but also the expertise and personalities of its staff. Fans of the show often come hoping to catch a glimpse of the stars—Rick Harrison, Corey "Big Hoss" Harrison, and Austin "Chumlee" Russell—who sometimes make appearances at the shop and interact with fans. The shop's staff are known for their deep knowledge of history, antiques, and collectibles, and they often share fascinating stories about the items on display.

In addition to the regular pawn shop operations, the Gold & Silver Pawn Shop has expanded its offerings to include a range of branded merchandise, including T-shirts, mugs, and other souvenirs featuring the "Pawn Stars" logo. The shop also hosts occasional events, including autograph sessions and special sales, making it an ever-evolving attraction.

Whether you're a fan of the show or simply curious about the world of pawnbroking, the Gold & Silver Pawn Shop offers a unique experience that combines history, pop culture, and the thrill of discovering something truly special. It's a place where every item has a story, and every visit offers the possibility of finding a hidden gem.

Hotels and Casinos

Bellagio Hotel and Casino

The Bellagio Hotel and Casino is one of the most luxurious and iconic resorts on the Las Vegas Strip. Opened in 1998 by MGM Resorts International, Bellagio is renowned for its elegance, sophistication, and world-class amenities. Inspired by the picturesque town of Bellagio in Italy's Lake Como region, the resort features Italian architecture, lush gardens, and a stunning 8.5-acre lake.

One of Bellagio's most famous attractions is the Fountains of Bellagio, a mesmerizing water show set to music and lights. The fountains are choreographed to perform a variety of routines, with water jets shooting up to 460 feet in the air. The show runs every 30 minutes during the day and every 15 minutes in the evening, offering a spectacular display that draws crowds of visitors.

Inside the resort, the Bellagio Conservatory & Botanical Gardens is another highlight. This indoor garden features elaborate seasonal displays created by a team of horticulturists and designers. Each display is unique, incorporating thousands of plants, flowers, and trees to create a visually stunning experience.

The Bellagio is also home to several fine dining restaurants, including Le Cirque, Picasso, and the Michelin-starred restaurant, Spago by Wolfgang Puck. These establishments offer exquisite cuisine and impeccable service, making Bellagio a top destination for food enthusiasts.

The casino at Bellagio is equally impressive, offering a wide range of gaming options, including poker, blackjack, roulette, and slot machines. The Bellagio Poker Room is particularly famous, hosting high-stakes games and attracting professional players from around the world.

In addition to gaming and dining, Bellagio offers luxurious accommodations with over 3,900 rooms and suites. The rooms are elegantly appointed, featuring modern amenities and stunning views of the Strip, the lake, or the mountains.

Bellagio also boasts a variety of entertainment options, including the world-famous Cirque du Soleil show "O," which combines acrobatics, synchronized swimming, and diving in a water-themed performance.

Overall, the Bellagio Hotel and Casino epitomizes luxury and sophistication, offering an unforgettable experience for visitors seeking the best of Las Vegas.

Caesars Palace

Caesars Palace is one of the most iconic and enduring resorts on the Las Vegas Strip, known for its opulent Roman-themed architecture and world-class entertainment. Opened in 1966, Caesars Palace has continually evolved to remain a premier destination for both luxury and excitement.

The resort's design is inspired by the grandeur of ancient Rome, featuring marble statues, ornate columns, and lavish decor. The Garden of the Gods Pool Oasis, with its seven stunning pools surrounded by classical statues and fountains, offers a luxurious retreat for guests looking to relax in style.

Caesars Palace is renowned for its entertainment offerings, particularly the Colosseum, a state-of-the-art theater that hosts some of the biggest names in music and entertainment. The Colosseum has been home to legendary residencies by artists like Celine Dion, Elton John, and Mariah Carey, providing unforgettable performances in an intimate setting.

The resort also boasts a wide range of dining options, from casual eateries to fine dining. Notable restaurants include Gordon Ramsay Hell's Kitchen, which offers a theatrical dining experience inspired by the hit TV show, and Restaurant Guy Savoy, a Michelin-starred restaurant offering exquisite French cuisine.

Caesars Palace's casino is one of the largest on the Strip, featuring an extensive selection of table games, slot machines, and a world-famous poker room. The casino's opulent design and lively atmosphere make it a popular destination for both casual gamblers and high rollers.

Shopping enthusiasts will find plenty to explore at The Forum Shops at Caesars, an upscale shopping mall with over 160 stores, including luxury brands like Gucci, Louis Vuitton, and Versace. The mall's design includes elaborate fountains, statues, and a stunning sky ceiling that changes from day to night, creating a unique shopping experience.

In addition to its entertainment, dining, and shopping options, Caesars Palace offers luxurious accommodations with over 4,000 rooms and suites. Each room is elegantly designed, featuring modern amenities and spectacular views of the Strip or the surrounding mountains.

Caesars Palace remains a symbol of luxury and entertainment, offering an unforgettable experience that combines the best of Las Vegas with the timeless grandeur of ancient Rome.

The Venetian Resort

The Venetian Resort is a luxurious and grandiose destination on the Las Vegas Strip, renowned for its elaborate design that captures the essence of Venice, Italy. Opened in 1999 by the Las Vegas Sands Corporation, the resort features stunning replicas of famous Venetian landmarks, including the Grand Canal, St. Mark's Square, and the Rialto Bridge.

One of the most unique attractions at The Venetian is the Grand Canal Shoppes, an upscale shopping mall designed to resemble the streets of Venice. The mall features cobblestone walkways, authentic Italian gondolas, and a picturesque canal winding through the property. Visitors can enjoy a romantic gondola ride with singing gondoliers, providing a quintessential Venetian experience in the heart of Las Vegas.

The Venetian is home to an array of fine dining options, offering a diverse range of cuisines from around the world. Notable restaurants include Delmonico Steakhouse by Emeril Lagasse, Bouchon by Thomas Keller, and CUT by Wolfgang Puck. Each restaurant provides an exceptional dining experience, combining exquisite cuisine with impeccable service.

The casino at The Venetian offers an extensive selection of gaming options, including table games, slot machines, and a luxurious poker room. The resort also features the TAO Nightclub, a popular nightlife destination known for its vibrant atmosphere and celebrity sightings.

In addition to its gaming and dining options, The Venetian is renowned for its luxurious accommodations. The resort boasts over 4,000 spacious suites, each elegantly designed with modern amenities and stunning views of the Strip or the surrounding area. The suites feature plush bedding, marble bathrooms, and separate living areas, providing a comfortable and opulent retreat for guests.

The Venetian also offers a variety of entertainment options, including the intimate Venetian Theatre, which hosts a range of performances from concerts to Broadway-style shows. The resort's partnership with Cirque du Soleil brings spectacular productions to the stage, captivating audiences with acrobatics, dance, and music.

Overall, The Venetian Resort offers a unique blend of luxury, entertainment, and cultural immersion. Its stunning architecture, world-class amenities, and exceptional service make it a must-visit destination for anyone seeking an unforgettable Las Vegas experience.

Wynn Las Vegas

Wynn Las Vegas is a premier luxury resort on the Las Vegas Strip, known for its elegant design, exceptional service, and world-class amenities. Opened in 2005 by developer Steve Wynn, the resort has set a new standard for luxury and sophistication in Las Vegas.

The resort's design is characterized by its sleek, curved facade and lush landscaping. The interior is equally impressive, featuring opulent decor, high-end finishes, and an array of artistic touches, including stunning floral displays and a large collection of fine art.

Wynn Las Vegas is home to several acclaimed dining establishments, offering a variety of culinary experiences. Notable restaurants include SW Steakhouse, which offers prime steaks and stunning views of the resort's Lake of Dreams; Mizumi, a Japanese restaurant known for its fresh sushi and teppanyaki; and Costa di Mare, which serves exquisite Italian seafood dishes. These restaurants, along with others at the resort, have earned Wynn Las Vegas a reputation as a top dining destination.

The resort's casino offers a luxurious gaming experience, with an extensive selection of table games, slot machines, and a high-limit salon. The casino's elegant design and attentive service create an inviting atmosphere for both casual gamblers and high rollers.

Wynn Las Vegas also features a variety of entertainment options, including the Wynn Theater, which hosts large-scale productions and performances by world-renowned artists. The Lake of Dreams, a stunning outdoor show set against a 40-foot waterfall, combines music, lights, and holographics to create a mesmerizing spectacle.

In addition to its gaming and entertainment options, Wynn Las Vegas offers luxurious accommodations with over 2,700 rooms and suites. Each room is elegantly designed, featuring modern amenities, plush bedding, and floor-to-ceiling windows with breathtaking views of the Strip or the resort's gardens.

The resort also boasts an array of recreational facilities, including an 18-hole championship golf course designed by Tom Fazio, a luxurious spa and salon, and multiple swimming pools surrounded by private cabanas. The Wynn Esplanade, an upscale shopping promenade, offers a selection of high-end boutiques, including Chanel, Louis Vuitton, and Rolex.

Overall, Wynn Las Vegas epitomizes luxury and sophistication, offering an unparalleled experience for guests seeking the best of Las Vegas. Its exceptional service, world-class amenities, and elegant design make it a standout destination on the Strip.

MGM Grand

MGM Grand, one of the largest and most iconic resorts on the Las Vegas Strip, opened in 1993 and has since become a landmark destination for visitors seeking the ultimate Las Vegas experience. With over 6,800 rooms, MGM Grand is one of the largest hotels in the world and offers a vast array of entertainment, dining, and gaming options.

The MGM Grand is renowned for its expansive casino, which spans over 170,000 square feet and features a wide range of gaming options, including slot machines, table games, and a bustling poker room. The casino's luxurious atmosphere and attentive service make it a popular destination for both casual players and high rollers.

One of the standout features of MGM Grand is its impressive lineup of entertainment options. The resort is home to the Grand Garden Arena, a premier venue that hosts major concerts, sporting events, and award shows. Additionally, MGM Grand is famous for its resident shows, including the spectacular Cirque du Soleil production "KÀ," which combines acrobatics, martial arts, and cutting-edge technology to create a mesmerizing performance.

Dining at MGM Grand is a culinary adventure, with an array of restaurants offering diverse cuisines from around the world. Notable dining establishments include Joel Robuchon, a Michelin three-star restaurant known for its exquisite French cuisine, and Hakkasan, which offers contemporary Cantonese dishes in a chic setting. The resort also features a variety of casual dining options, ensuring that there is something to suit every palate.

Accommodations at MGM Grand are luxurious and well-appointed, with rooms and suites offering modern amenities and stunning views of the Las Vegas skyline. The resort also features several exclusive suites and villas, providing an opulent experience for guests seeking the highest level of luxury.

For those looking to unwind, MGM Grand offers multiple pools, including the famous Grand Pool Complex, which features four swimming pools, three whirlpools, and a lazy river. The resort also boasts a luxurious spa and fitness center, offering a range of treatments and services to help guests relax and rejuvenate.

Overall, MGM Grand epitomizes the excitement and grandeur of Las Vegas, offering a comprehensive resort experience that caters to a wide range of interests and tastes.

ARIA Resort & Casino

ARIA Resort & Casino, located in the heart of the Las Vegas Strip, is a contemporary luxury resort known for its cutting-edge design, sophisticated atmosphere, and exceptional amenities. Opened in 2009 as part of the CityCenter complex, ARIA has quickly established itself as a premier destination for travelers seeking a modern and upscale Las Vegas experience.

One of the defining features of ARIA is its innovative architecture and sustainable design. The resort's sleek, curvilinear towers are clad in glass, creating a striking visual presence on the Strip. ARIA is also a LEED Gold certified property, reflecting its commitment to environmental sustainability through energy-efficient systems, water conservation, and green building practices.

The casino at ARIA spans 150,000 square feet and offers a wide variety of gaming options, including slot machines, table games, and a high-limit room. The casino's contemporary design and high-tech features, such as personalized gaming experiences and interactive touchscreens, create a unique and engaging atmosphere for guests.

ARIA is home to several world-class dining establishments, offering a diverse range of culinary experiences. Notable restaurants include Jean Georges Steakhouse, which serves prime steaks and seafood in a stylish setting, and Carbone, an upscale Italian-American restaurant known for its classic dishes and retro ambiance. For a more casual dining experience, ARIA offers a variety of options, including a bustling food court and several cafes.

Accommodations at ARIA are designed with modern luxury in mind, featuring sleek decor, advanced technology, and stunning views of the city. The resort's rooms and suites are equipped with state-of-the-art amenities, such as automated controls for lighting and temperature, as well as floor-to-ceiling windows that offer panoramic vistas of the Las Vegas skyline.

ARIA also boasts an array of recreational facilities, including three distinctive pools, a luxurious spa and salon, and a state-of-the-art fitness center. The resort's pool area features private cabanas, hot tubs, and a lively pool bar, providing the perfect setting for relaxation and socializing.

Entertainment at ARIA includes resident shows, such as the critically acclaimed "Zarkana" by Cirque du Soleil, as well as a variety of live performances and events. The resort is also home to several high-end boutiques and retail shops, offering a curated selection of fashion, jewelry, and accessories.

Overall, ARIA Resort & Casino offers a sophisticated and contemporary take on the classic Las Vegas experience, combining luxurious accommodations, exceptional dining, and innovative entertainment in a stunning modern setting.

The Cosmopolitan of Las Vegas

The Cosmopolitan of Las Vegas, often simply referred to as The Cosmopolitan, is a chic and modern resort known for its stylish design, upscale amenities, and vibrant atmosphere. Opened in 2010, The Cosmopolitan has quickly become one of the trendiest destinations on the Las Vegas Strip, attracting a fashionable and cosmopolitan crowd.

One of the standout features of The Cosmopolitan is its unique architectural design. The resort's two sleek towers are adorned with striking digital displays and artistic installations, creating a visually captivating presence. Inside, the resort's decor blends contemporary luxury with artistic flair, featuring eclectic artwork, modern furnishings, and innovative design elements.

The Cosmopolitan offers a variety of luxurious accommodations, including spacious rooms, suites, and penthouses. Each room is elegantly designed with modern amenities, such as marble bathrooms, plush bedding, and private balconies offering stunning views of the Las Vegas skyline. The resort's unique terrace suites are particularly popular, providing guests with expansive outdoor spaces to enjoy the city's vibrant energy.

Dining at The Cosmopolitan is a culinary adventure, with a diverse range of restaurants offering world-class cuisine. Notable dining establishments include Estiatorio Milos, a Mediterranean seafood restaurant known for its fresh ingredients and elegant ambiance, and Momofuku, which offers innovative Asian-inspired dishes by celebrity chef David Chang. The resort also features the trendy Beauty & Essex, an upscale eatery that combines fine dining with a speakeasy vibe.

The casino at The Cosmopolitan spans 100,000 square feet and offers a wide variety of gaming options, including slot machines, table games, and a high-limit lounge. The casino's modern design and vibrant atmosphere make it a popular destination for both casual gamblers and high-stakes players.

The Cosmopolitan is renowned for its vibrant nightlife, offering a variety of bars, lounges, and nightclubs. The resort's marquee nightclub, Marquee, is one of the most popular nightlife venues in Las Vegas, featuring top DJs, a lively dance floor, and a rooftop pool area. Other notable nightlife spots include The Chandelier, a three-story bar encased in a shimmering crystal chandelier, and the sophisticated Vesper Bar.

In addition to its gaming and nightlife options, The Cosmopolitan offers a range of recreational facilities, including three distinct pool experiences. The Boulevard Pool offers a lively social scene with cabanas, daybeds, and stunning views of the Strip, while the Bamboo Pool provides a more tranquil retreat. The Chelsea Pool is an intimate, private pool area for hotel guests.

Overall, The Cosmopolitan of Las Vegas combines contemporary luxury, artistic design, and a vibrant social scene, offering a unique and unforgettable Las Vegas experience.

Mandalay Bay Resort and Casino is a sprawling, luxurious destination located at the southern end of the Las Vegas Strip. Opened in 1999, Mandalay Bay is known for its tropical theme, extensive amenities, and world-class entertainment options, making it a favorite among visitors seeking a comprehensive resort experience.

One of the most distinctive features of Mandalay Bay is its expansive pool complex, known as Mandalay Bay Beach. This 11-acre aquatic playground features a large wave pool, a lazy river, and a sandy beach with real sand, creating a tropical oasis in the middle of the desert. The pool area also includes several swimming pools, cabanas, and the adults-only Moorea Beach Club, which offers a more exclusive and relaxed atmosphere.

The casino at Mandalay Bay spans 135,000 square feet and offers a wide range of gaming options, including slot machines, table games, and a dedicated poker room. The casino's vibrant atmosphere and diverse gaming offerings make it a popular destination for both casual and serious gamblers.

Dining at Mandalay Bay is a culinary delight, with an array of restaurants offering diverse cuisines from around the world. Notable dining establishments include Aureole, a fine dining restaurant known for its wine tower and innovative American cuisine, and StripSteak by Michael Mina, which offers prime steaks and seafood in an elegant setting. The resort also features a variety of casual dining options, including the popular Border Grill, which serves modern Mexican fare.

Mandalay Bay is renowned for its entertainment options, including the Mandalay Bay Events Center, which hosts major concerts, sporting events, and award shows. The resort is also home to the House of Blues, a famous live music venue that features performances by top artists in a range of genres. Additionally, Mandalay Bay hosts the Cirque du Soleil show "Michael Jackson ONE," a spectacular tribute to the King of Pop.

In addition to its entertainment and dining offerings, Mandalay Bay features luxurious accommodations with over 3,200 rooms and suites. Each room is elegantly designed with modern amenities, providing a comfortable and stylish retreat for guests. The resort also offers the exclusive Four Seasons Hotel Las Vegas, located on the top floors of Mandalay Bay, providing an even higher level of luxury and personalized service.

Mandalay Bay is also home to several unique attractions, including the Shark Reef Aquarium, which houses over 2,000 marine animals and features interactive exhibits and underwater tunnels. The resort's extensive convention center and meeting facilities make it a popular destination for business travelers and large events.

Overall, Mandalay Bay Resort and Casino offers a diverse and comprehensive Las Vegas experience, combining luxurious accommodations, world-class entertainment, and exceptional dining in a tropical-inspired setting.

Luxor Hotel & Casino

Luxor Hotel & Casino is one of the most distinctive and visually striking resorts on the Las Vegas Strip. Opened in 1993, the Luxor is designed to evoke the grandeur and mystery of ancient Egypt, featuring a 30-story pyramid as its main structure, complete with a massive sphinx and an obelisk at its entrance.

The pyramid itself is an architectural marvel, with a sleek black exterior and a beam of light that shoots from its apex into the night sky, visible from miles away. This beam, known as the Luxor Sky Beam, is the strongest beam of light in the world, making the Luxor an iconic part of the Las Vegas skyline.

Inside the Luxor, the Egyptian theme continues with decor and design elements that transport guests to another time and place. The atrium, which is the largest in the world, is a vast open space filled with themed exhibits, statues, and replicas of ancient artifacts. The resort features over 4,400 rooms and suites, many of which are located within the pyramid itself, offering unique angled views and spacious interiors.

The Luxor's casino spans 120,000 square feet and offers a wide range of gaming options, including slot machines, table games, and a dedicated poker room. The casino's vibrant atmosphere and themed decor enhance the overall gaming experience, making it a popular destination for both casual players and serious gamblers.

Entertainment at the Luxor is top-notch, with several resident shows that draw large crowds. "Fantasy" is a popular adult revue that combines music, dance, and comedy, while "Carrot Top" features the renowned comedian known for his energetic and prop-filled performances. The Blue

Man Group also has a residency at the Luxor, offering a unique blend of music, comedy, and multimedia performance art.

Dining options at the Luxor are diverse, ranging from casual eateries to fine dining. TENDER Steakhouse offers prime cuts of beef and fresh seafood in an elegant setting, while Diablo's Cantina serves up vibrant Mexican cuisine and cocktails.

The resort also features a variety of nightlife options, including the popular LAX Nightclub and several bars and lounges. Additionally, the Luxor is home to the immersive Titanic: The Artifact Exhibition and Bodies... The Exhibition, both of which provide fascinating and educational experiences.

Overall, Luxor Hotel & Casino combines the allure of ancient Egypt with modern luxury and entertainment, making it a unique and memorable destination on the Las Vegas Strip.

Excalibur Hotel & Casino

Excalibur Hotel & Casino, opened in 1990, is a themed resort on the Las Vegas Strip that transports visitors to the medieval era of knights and castles. Designed to resemble a grand castle complete with turrets, drawbridges, and a moat, Excalibur offers a whimsical and family-friendly experience amidst the glitz and glamour of Las Vegas.

The exterior of Excalibur is instantly recognizable, with its colorful castle towers and medieval-themed facade. Inside, the theme continues with decor and design elements that evoke the days of King Arthur and the Knights of the Round Table. The resort features over 4,000 rooms and suites, providing comfortable accommodations with modern amenities while maintaining a touch of the castle theme.

The casino at Excalibur spans 100,000 square feet and offers a wide variety of gaming options, including slot machines, table games, and a poker room. The casino's lively and welcoming atmosphere makes it a popular destination for both casual gamblers and experienced players. For those looking to try their luck, Excalibur also offers an array of daily tournaments and special gaming events.

Excalibur is well-known for its entertainment offerings, particularly its medieval-themed shows. The Tournament of Kings is a dinner show that features jousting knights, epic battles, and a feast fit for royalty. Guests are seated in an arena-style setting and encouraged to cheer for their knight, creating an immersive and interactive experience. The show is one of the most popular family-friendly attractions in Las Vegas.

In addition to the Tournament of Kings, Excalibur hosts a variety of other entertainment options. The resort's Thunder from Down Under is a popular male revue that attracts bachelorette parties and groups looking for a fun night out. The Australian Bee Gees Show offers a tribute to the legendary band with an energetic and nostalgic performance.

Dining at Excalibur includes a range of options to suit all tastes and budgets. The Camelot Steakhouse provides a fine dining experience with premium cuts of beef and seafood, while The Buffet at Excalibur offers a casual and extensive dining option with a variety of cuisines. For a quick bite, the food court features popular fast-food chains and quick-service restaurants.

Excalibur also caters to families with its Fun Dungeon, an arcade and gaming area that includes carnival games, video games, and a variety of activities for children and adults alike. The resort's pool area features multiple swimming pools, including a separate kids' pool and a relaxing whirlpool spa.

Overall, Excalibur Hotel & Casino offers a unique blend of medieval charm and modern amenities, making it an ideal destination for families and visitors seeking a playful and entertaining Las Vegas experience.

Museums and Cultural Institutions

The Neon Museum

The Neon Museum, often referred to as the "Neon Boneyard," is a must-visit attraction in Las Vegas that celebrates the city's vibrant history through its iconic neon signs. Established in 1996, the museum is dedicated to collecting, preserving, and exhibiting these fascinating relics of Las Vegas's past.

Located just north of the Las Vegas Strip, the Neon Museum features an outdoor exhibition space where visitors can stroll through a collection of more than 200 retired signs. These signs, which once adorned casinos, hotels, and other businesses, provide a nostalgic glimpse into the city's glamorous history. The museum's main collection is housed in the Neon Boneyard, a two-acre lot filled with signs that range from small, simple designs to massive, elaborate displays.

Each sign in the collection has a story to tell, reflecting the evolution of design, technology, and culture in Las Vegas. Highlights include the iconic signs from the Stardust, Sahara, and Moulin Rouge, as well as pieces from lesser-known but historically significant establishments. The museum offers guided tours that provide in-depth insights into the history and significance of each sign, making the experience both educational and entertaining.

In addition to the Boneyard, the Neon Museum features the restored lobby shell of the La Concha Motel, which serves as the visitor center. This mid-century modern structure, designed by architect Paul Revere Williams, adds to the museum's historical ambiance.

The Neon Museum also hosts special events, including evening tours and light shows, where some of the restored signs are illuminated, creating a magical atmosphere. The museum's commitment to preservation extends to its Neon Signs Project, which aims to restore and reinstall signs on their original locations throughout the city.

Overall, the Neon Museum is a unique and captivating destination that offers a deep dive into the dazzling visual history of Las Vegas. It provides an opportunity to appreciate the artistry and craftsmanship of neon signs while reflecting on the city's ever-evolving identity.

The Mob Museum, officially known as the National Museum of Organized Crime and Law Enforcement, offers a fascinating and comprehensive look into the history of organized crime and its impact on American society. Located in downtown Las Vegas, the museum is housed in a historic former federal courthouse and U.S. Post Office building, adding to its authenticity and historical significance.

Opened in 2012, The Mob Museum presents a detailed narrative of the rise and fall of organized crime in the United States, with a particular focus on its influence in Las Vegas. The museum's exhibits are meticulously curated, featuring interactive displays, multimedia presentations, and a vast collection of artifacts, photographs, and documents.

One of the museum's key attractions is the courtroom where the Kefauver Committee hearings were held in the 1950s. These hearings were part of a nationwide investigation into organized crime, and their findings played a crucial role in shaping public perception and law enforcement policies. Visitors can sit in the actual courtroom and watch video excerpts from the hearings, gaining a firsthand understanding of this pivotal moment in history.

The Mob Museum's exhibits cover a wide range of topics, from the origins of the mafia and the Prohibition era to the infamous mobsters who shaped the criminal underworld. Notable displays include personal items belonging to notorious figures like Al Capone, Bugsy Siegel, and John Gotti, as well as weapons, wiretapping equipment, and other crime-related artifacts.

The museum also explores the law enforcement side of the story, highlighting the efforts of the FBI, local police, and other agencies to combat organized crime. Interactive exhibits allow visitors to experience the challenges and dangers faced by law enforcement officers, such as participating in a simulated raid or wiretapping operation.

In addition to its permanent exhibits, The Mob Museum hosts temporary exhibitions, educational programs, and special events that delve deeper into specific aspects of organized crime and its legacy. The museum also features a speakeasy and distillery in the basement, where visitors can enjoy Prohibition-era cocktails and learn about the history of bootlegging.

Overall, The Mob Museum provides a riveting and immersive experience that sheds light on the dark and complex history of organized crime in

America. It is a must-visit for anyone interested in understanding the interplay between crime, law enforcement, and society.

Las Vegas Natural History Museum

The Las Vegas Natural History Museum, located just north of downtown Las Vegas, offers a captivating journey through natural history, providing educational and engaging exhibits for visitors of all ages. Established in 1991, the museum aims to inspire a passion for science and nature by showcasing a diverse collection of exhibits that cover various aspects of the natural world.

One of the museum's highlights is its extensive display of prehistoric life, featuring life-sized replicas of dinosaurs and other ancient creatures. The Dinosaur Gallery includes impressive models of a Tyrannosaurus rex, Triceratops, and other iconic dinosaurs, offering visitors a glimpse into the fascinating world of these prehistoric giants. Interactive exhibits and hands-on activities help bring the prehistoric era to life, making it an exciting experience for children and adults alike.

The Las Vegas Natural History Museum also features an array of exhibits on ancient civilizations. The Egyptian Exhibit is particularly notable, with a detailed replica of the tomb of Tutankhamun, complete with artifacts, hieroglyphics, and a life-sized statue of the young pharaoh. This exhibit provides an immersive look into the rich history and culture of ancient Egypt.

Another key attraction is the Marine Life Gallery, which showcases the diverse ecosystems of the world's oceans. The gallery includes a variety of marine specimens, from colorful coral reefs and exotic fish to larger sea creatures like sharks and rays. An interactive touch tank allows visitors to get up close and personal with some of the marine life, providing a hands-on educational experience.

The museum also houses exhibits on Nevada's natural history, highlighting the region's unique geology, flora, and fauna. Visitors can explore the rich biodiversity of the Mojave Desert and learn about the various species that inhabit this arid landscape. The Wildlife Gallery features dioramas of animals from around the world, including African savannas and North American forests.

In addition to its permanent exhibits, the Las Vegas Natural History Museum hosts temporary exhibitions, educational programs, and special events throughout the year. These activities aim to engage the community and promote a deeper understanding of the natural world.

Overall, the Las Vegas Natural History Museum is a valuable educational resource that offers a diverse and enriching experience. It provides a fun and informative destination for families, students, and anyone interested in exploring the wonders of natural history.

Nevada State Museum, Las Vegas

The Nevada State Museum, Las Vegas, located in the Springs Preserve, offers an in-depth exploration of the rich history and cultural heritage of Nevada. Opened in 1982, the museum is dedicated to preserving and interpreting the natural and cultural history of the state, providing visitors with a comprehensive understanding of Nevada's past and present.

The museum's exhibits cover a wide range of topics, from the geological formations that shaped the region to the cultural and social developments that have defined its history. One of the museum's key attractions is the "Nevada: A People and Place Through Time" exhibit, which takes visitors on a chronological journey through the state's history. This exhibit includes detailed dioramas, interactive displays, and a wealth of artifacts that bring Nevada's story to life.

A significant focus of the museum is the history of Las Vegas and its development from a small desert town to a bustling metropolis. Exhibits highlight the early days of Las Vegas, including the arrival of the railroad, the construction of the Hoover Dam, and the rise of the gaming and entertainment industries. Visitors can explore the cultural impact of these developments and gain insights into the city's unique identity.

The Nevada State Museum also features an extensive collection of artifacts from the state's mining history. The "Mining in Nevada" exhibit showcases tools, equipment, and minerals that illustrate the importance of mining in Nevada's economic and social development. This exhibit provides a fascinating look at the challenges and innovations of the mining industry and its enduring legacy in the state.

Natural history is another key component of the museum, with exhibits that explore Nevada's diverse ecosystems and wildlife. The "Nevada's Natural Heritage" exhibit features specimens of native plants and animals, as well as information on the state's geological history. Visitors can learn about the unique flora and fauna of the Mojave Desert and other regions, gaining a deeper appreciation for Nevada's natural environment.

In addition to its permanent exhibits, the Nevada State Museum hosts temporary exhibitions, educational programs, and special events. These activities aim to engage the community and provide opportunities for lifelong learning. The museum also features a research library and archives, offering valuable resources for scholars and history enthusiasts.

Overall, the Nevada State Museum, Las Vegas, is a vital cultural institution that offers a comprehensive and engaging look at the history and heritage of Nevada. It is a must-visit destination for anyone interested in exploring the rich and diverse stories that have shaped the state.

DISCOVERY Children's Museum

The DISCOVERY Children's Museum in Las Vegas is a premier educational and interactive destination designed to inspire a love of learning in children of all ages. Located in Symphony Park, adjacent to The Smith Center for the Performing Arts, the museum spans three floors and 58,000 square feet, offering a wide range of exhibits and activities that promote exploration, creativity, and critical thinking.

Opened in 1990 and relocated to its current state-of-the-art facility in 2013, the DISCOVERY Children's Museum is designed to be both educational and fun. The museum's exhibits cover various themes, including science, art, culture, and early childhood development. Each exhibit is hands-on and interactive, encouraging children to engage actively with the material and explore their interests.

One of the most popular exhibits is the Eco City, which allows children to explore a miniature city complete with a bank, grocery store, airport, and construction site. Here, kids can role-play and learn about different careers, financial literacy, and community roles in a fun and immersive environment.

The Water World exhibit teaches children about the properties of water through engaging activities. Kids can experiment with water flow, learn about the water cycle, and explore the impact of water on the environment. This exhibit combines play with science education, making complex concepts accessible and enjoyable for young learners.

For the youngest visitors, Toddler Town provides a safe and stimulating environment where children under five can explore and play. This area is designed to support early childhood development through activities that promote motor skills, cognitive development, and social interaction.

The museum also features traveling exhibits that rotate throughout the year, bringing new and exciting educational opportunities to the community. These exhibits cover a wide range of topics, ensuring there is always something new to discover at the museum.

In addition to its exhibits, the DISCOVERY Children's Museum offers a variety of educational programs, workshops, and camps. These programs are designed to enhance the learning experience and provide children with additional opportunities to explore their interests and develop new skills.

The DISCOVERY Children's Museum is a vibrant and dynamic place that fosters a lifelong love of learning. Its interactive exhibits and engaging programs make it a must-visit destination for families in Las Vegas, providing a fun and educational experience that children will remember for years to come.

Madame Tussauds Las Vegas

Madame Tussauds Las Vegas, located at The Venetian Resort, is a world-famous wax museum that offers visitors an up-close and personal experience with lifelike wax figures of their favorite celebrities, historical figures, and iconic characters. Opened in 1999, this interactive attraction is part of the renowned Madame Tussauds franchise, known for its meticulous attention to detail and high-quality craftsmanship.

The museum features a diverse collection of wax figures, each created by skilled artists who use a combination of traditional sculpting techniques and modern technology to achieve astonishing realism. Visitors can explore themed exhibits and pose for photos with wax figures of Hollywood stars, music legends, sports heroes, and influential political figures.

One of the most popular sections of Madame Tussauds Las Vegas is the "Music Icons" exhibit, where guests can meet and snap selfies with lifelike figures of pop stars like Michael Jackson, Beyoncé, and Elvis Presley. The museum also includes interactive elements, such as karaoke booths and dance floors, allowing visitors to immerse themselves in the world of music.

The "Marvel Super Heroes" exhibit is another highlight, featuring figures of beloved characters like Spider-Man, Iron Man, and the Hulk. This area includes a thrilling 4D cinema experience, where visitors can enjoy an action-packed Marvel adventure with special effects that bring the story to life.

In the "Las Vegas Legends" exhibit, guests can encounter figures of iconic entertainers who have left their mark on the city, such as Frank Sinatra, Wayne Newton, and Liberace. This section celebrates the rich entertainment history of Las Vegas and its legendary performers.

Madame Tussauds Las Vegas also offers seasonal exhibits and special events, ensuring that there is always something new and exciting to see. The museum's interactive nature and lifelike figures make it a popular destination for tourists and locals alike, providing a unique and memorable experience.

Overall, Madame Tussauds Las Vegas offers a fun and engaging way to get up close with famous faces from around the world. Its meticulously crafted wax figures and interactive exhibits make it a must-visit attraction on the Las Vegas Strip, providing entertainment and photo opportunities for visitors of all ages.

Bellagio Gallery of Fine Art

The Bellagio Gallery of Fine Art, located within the Bellagio Hotel and Casino, is a premier art venue in Las Vegas that showcases a rotating selection of artworks from some of the world's most renowned museums and private collections. Since its opening in 1998, the gallery has become a cultural gem on the Las Vegas Strip, offering visitors an opportunity to experience high-quality art in an elegant setting.

The gallery's exhibitions cover a wide range of artistic styles and periods, featuring works by both classical and contemporary artists. Past exhibitions have included masterpieces by legendary artists such as Pablo Picasso, Claude Monet, Andy Warhol, and Georgia O'Keeffe. These exhibitions are carefully curated to provide an enriching and educational experience, allowing visitors to explore the diverse world of visual art.

One of the key features of the Bellagio Gallery of Fine Art is its intimate and thoughtfully designed space. The gallery's serene atmosphere and sophisticated layout create an ideal environment for appreciating art. Soft lighting, elegant decor, and detailed exhibit descriptions enhance the viewing experience, allowing visitors to engage deeply with the artworks on display.

In addition to its rotating exhibitions, the Bellagio Gallery of Fine Art offers a variety of educational programs and special events. These include artist talks, guided tours, and lectures that provide additional insights into the works and themes of the current exhibitions. The gallery also collaborates with other cultural institutions to bring unique and exclusive art experiences to Las Vegas.

The Bellagio Gallery of Fine Art is committed to making art accessible to a wide audience, offering discounted admission for students, seniors, and Nevada residents. The gallery's location within the Bellagio Hotel and Casino makes it a convenient and enriching cultural stop for tourists exploring the Las Vegas Strip.

The gallery's dedication to showcasing exceptional art has earned it a reputation as a leading art destination in Las Vegas. It provides a welcome respite from the city's vibrant entertainment scene, offering a space for reflection, inspiration, and appreciation of fine art.

Overall, the Bellagio Gallery of Fine Art is a must-visit destination for art enthusiasts and anyone looking to experience the cultural side of Las Vegas. Its high-quality exhibitions, educational programs, and elegant setting make it a standout attraction that enriches the city's diverse array of offerings.

Pinball Hall of Fame

The Pinball Hall of Fame is a unique and nostalgic attraction in Las Vegas, dedicated to the preservation and enjoyment of classic pinball machines. Located just off the Las Vegas Strip, this museum is a haven for pinball enthusiasts and casual visitors alike, offering a fascinating glimpse into the history of this beloved arcade game.

Established by the Las Vegas Pinball Collectors Club, the Pinball Hall of Fame first opened its doors in 2006 and has since grown to house an impressive collection of over 200 pinball machines. The machines range from vintage models dating back to the 1950s to more contemporary examples from the 1990s and beyond. Each machine is meticulously restored and maintained, ensuring that visitors can experience them in their original glory.

The Pinball Hall of Fame operates as a nonprofit organization, with all proceeds from the games going to local charities. This charitable mission adds an extra layer of goodwill to the nostalgic fun, making each visit not only enjoyable but also meaningful.

Visitors to the Pinball Hall of Fame can play any of the machines on display, with games costing between 25 cents and a dollar. This interactive element allows guests to experience the sights, sounds, and tactile sensations of playing a real pinball machine, making it a hit for both adults reliving their childhood memories and younger visitors discovering the magic of pinball for the first time.

The museum is also home to several rare and unusual machines, some of which are unique to the Pinball Hall of Fame. These include early electro-mechanical models, as well as modern, highly sophisticated machines with elaborate themes and complex gameplay.

In addition to its extensive collection of pinball machines, the Pinball Hall of Fame features a selection of vintage arcade games, adding to the retro gaming experience. The museum's unassuming, warehouse-like setting creates an authentic and laid-back atmosphere where the focus remains squarely on the games themselves.

Overall, the Pinball Hall of Fame offers a delightful and immersive journey into the world of pinball. Its extensive collection, interactive play opportunities, and charitable mission make it a must-visit destination for anyone seeking a unique and entertaining experience in Las Vegas.

National Atomic Testing Museum

The National Atomic Testing Museum in Las Vegas offers a compelling and educational exploration of the history of nuclear testing in the United States, particularly focusing on the Nevada Test Site. Located just a few miles from the Las Vegas Strip, the museum provides a comprehensive look at the science, history, and impact of nuclear testing on both a national and global scale.

Opened in 2005, the National Atomic Testing Museum is an affiliate of the Smithsonian Institution and features a wide array of exhibits, artifacts, and interactive displays. The museum's mission is to preserve and present the history of nuclear testing, highlighting its role in the Cold War and its ongoing legacy.

One of the museum's most striking exhibits is the Ground Zero Theater, which simulates the experience of witnessing an atomic bomb test. This immersive exhibit uses sound, light, and visual effects to recreate the sights and sounds of a nuclear explosion, providing visitors with a visceral understanding of the power and impact of these tests.

The museum's permanent exhibits cover a broad range of topics, including the development of nuclear weapons, the scientific principles behind atomic energy, and the geopolitical context of the Cold War. Visitors can explore detailed displays about the Nevada Test Site, where over 900 nuclear tests were conducted between 1951 and 1992. The exhibits include photographs, historical documents, and personal stories from those who worked at the test site.

In addition to its historical exhibits, the National Atomic Testing Museum also addresses contemporary issues related to nuclear energy and proliferation. Interactive displays and multimedia presentations help visitors understand the ongoing challenges and debates surrounding nuclear technology.

The museum is home to several rare and significant artifacts, including nuclear test devices, Geiger counters, and protective gear used by scientists and military personnel. These artifacts provide a tangible connection to the history of nuclear testing and illustrate the technological advancements made over the decades.

The National Atomic Testing Museum also hosts special exhibitions, educational programs, and public lectures, offering visitors additional opportunities to engage with the subject matter. These events often feature experts in the field of nuclear science and history, providing valuable insights and fostering a deeper understanding of the complexities of nuclear testing.

Overall, the National Atomic Testing Museum is a thought-provoking and informative destination that offers a unique perspective on one of the most significant aspects of modern history. Its comprehensive exhibits, immersive experiences, and educational programs make it a must-visit for anyone interested in science, history, and the impact of nuclear technology.

The Marjorie Barrick Museum of Art, located on the University of Nevada, Las Vegas (UNLV) campus, is a vibrant cultural institution dedicated to contemporary art and the preservation of regional artistic heritage. Originally established in 1967 as a natural history museum, the Marjorie Barrick Museum of Art has evolved to become a prominent venue for art exhibitions, community engagement, and cultural education in Las Vegas.

The museum's mission is to inspire and educate through the visual arts, offering a dynamic range of exhibitions that showcase the work of both established and emerging artists. The Marjorie Barrick Museum of Art places a strong emphasis on contemporary art, particularly works that reflect the diverse cultural landscape of the American Southwest and the broader global context.

One of the key features of the museum is its commitment to supporting local and regional artists. The museum regularly collaborates with artists from Nevada and the surrounding areas, providing a platform for them to present their work and engage with the community. These exhibitions often explore themes relevant to the region, such as identity, migration, and the environment, offering visitors a deeper understanding of the local cultural and artistic landscape.

The Marjorie Barrick Museum of Art also hosts a variety of temporary exhibitions featuring national and international artists. These exhibitions cover a wide range of media, including painting, sculpture, photography, video, and installation art. The museum's diverse programming ensures that there is always something new and exciting for visitors to experience.

In addition to its exhibitions, the museum offers a robust schedule of educational programs and public events. These include artist talks, panel discussions, workshops, and guided tours, all designed to foster a deeper engagement with the art on display. The museum's educational initiatives aim to make contemporary art accessible and relevant to a broad audience, including students, educators, and the general public.

The museum's location on the UNLV campus allows for a strong connection with the academic community, fostering collaborations between artists, scholars, and students. This synergy enhances the museum's role as a center for cultural and intellectual exchange.

Overall, the Marjorie Barrick Museum of Art is a vital cultural hub in Las Vegas, offering a rich and varied program of contemporary art exhibitions and educational activities. Its commitment to supporting local artists and engaging with the community makes it a unique and valuable institution, contributing to the vibrant cultural landscape of the region.

Theaters and Performances

The Colosseum at Caesars Palace

The Colosseum at Caesars Palace is one of the premier entertainment venues on the Las Vegas Strip, known for hosting legendary performers and spectacular shows. Opened in 2003, this state-of-the-art theater was initially built for Celine Dion's groundbreaking residency, "A New Day...," and has since become a home for some of the biggest names in music and entertainment.

The Colosseum's design was inspired by the ancient Roman architecture of its namesake, featuring a grand facade and a luxurious, modern interior. The theater seats approximately 4,300 guests and is renowned for its excellent acoustics and unobstructed sightlines, ensuring an intimate and immersive experience for every audience member.

Over the years, The Colosseum has hosted an impressive lineup of resident performers, including Celine Dion, Elton John, Mariah Carey, Rod Stewart, and Reba McEntire. These residencies have set new standards for live performances in Las Vegas, combining state-of-the-art technology with world-class talent to create unforgettable shows.

The theater's advanced technical capabilities allow for stunning visual and audio effects, with an expansive stage, high-definition LED screens, and a sophisticated sound system. These features enhance the performances, making them some of the most visually and sonically impressive shows on the Strip.

In addition to its resident shows, The Colosseum also hosts one-off concerts, comedy acts, and special events, providing a diverse range of entertainment options. This versatility has solidified its reputation as a top venue for both performers and audiences alike.

The Colosseum at Caesars Palace is more than just a theater; it is a symbol of Las Vegas's commitment to top-tier entertainment. Its blend of architectural grandeur, cutting-edge technology, and exceptional performances make it a must-visit destination for anyone seeking a world-class entertainment experience in Las Vegas.

Zumanity Theater (Cirque du Soleil)

Zumanity Theater, located at New York-New York Hotel & Casino, was home to the Cirque du Soleil production "Zumanity," an adult-themed show that explored the sensual side of human nature. Running from 2003 until its closure in 2020, "Zumanity" was a daring departure from Cirque du Soleil's typical family-friendly offerings, blending cabaret, burlesque, and acrobatics into a provocative and captivating performance.

The theater itself was designed to complement the show's intimate and sensuous atmosphere, with a cozy seating arrangement that brought audiences close to the action. The venue accommodated approximately 1,200 guests, creating a personal and immersive experience that allowed the performers to interact directly with the audience.

"Zumanity" featured a diverse cast of performers, including contortionists, aerialists, dancers, and comedians, each bringing their unique talents to the stage. The show celebrated love, desire, and human connection through a series of vignettes that ranged from playful and humorous to deeply emotional and erotic. The use of elaborate costumes, imaginative set designs, and evocative music further enhanced the overall experience, making "Zumanity" a feast for the senses.

The theater's design included plush seating, rich drapery, and warm lighting, all contributing to the show's seductive ambiance. This intimate setting allowed the audience to feel like they were part of the performance, breaking down the traditional barriers between performers and spectators.

Although "Zumanity" has closed, the theater remains a symbol of Cirque du Soleil's innovative approach to live entertainment. The show pushed boundaries and challenged conventions, creating a unique and memorable experience for those who attended. The legacy of "Zumanity" lives on as a testament to the diversity and creativity of Cirque du Soleil's productions.

Overall, Zumanity Theater provided an exceptional venue for a show that redefined the Las Vegas entertainment scene. Its combination of intimate design, world-class performances, and bold themes made it a standout attraction on the Strip.

The Blue Man Group Theater, located at Luxor Hotel and Casino, is home to one of the most unique and innovative shows on the Las Vegas Strip. Blue Man Group, known for its eccentric blend of music, comedy, and multimedia performances, has captivated audiences worldwide since its inception in 1991. The Las Vegas production offers a high-energy, immersive experience that leaves audiences both entertained and inspired.

The theater itself is designed to enhance the Blue Man Group experience, featuring a modern and dynamic layout that includes state-of-the-art lighting, sound, and video systems. The seating arrangement ensures that every audience member has an excellent view of the stage, allowing them to fully engage with the show's visual and auditory elements.

The Blue Man Group show is characterized by its three bald, blue-painted performers who communicate solely through gestures and actions, creating a universal language that transcends cultural and linguistic barriers. The performance combines elements of percussion, technology, and visual art, resulting in a sensory-rich experience that is both thought-provoking and entertaining.

One of the hallmarks of the Blue Man Group show is its interactive nature. The performers frequently involve audience members in the act, creating spontaneous and unpredictable moments that add to the show's excitement. This interaction, combined with the use of inventive props and vibrant color schemes, ensures that no two performances are exactly alike.

The theater's advanced technical capabilities play a crucial role in the show, with cutting-edge visual effects, LED screens, and an immersive sound system that envelops the audience. These features, along with the Blue Man Group's signature use of PVC pipes and other unconventional instruments, create a multi-sensory experience that is unlike any other show in Las Vegas.

In addition to its nightly performances, the Blue Man Group Theater occasionally hosts special events and themed shows, offering fans new ways to experience the creativity and innovation of the Blue Man Group.

Overall, the Blue Man Group Theater at Luxor provides a perfect setting for a show that defies categorization. Its combination of cutting-edge technology, interactive performance, and artistic ingenuity makes it a must-see attraction for anyone visiting Las Vegas.

The Mirage Volcano, located in front of The Mirage Hotel and Casino on the Las Vegas Strip, is one of the city's most iconic and long-standing attractions. Since its debut in 1989, the volcano has captivated millions of visitors with its spectacular eruptions of fire, water, and light, providing a mesmerizing display of nature's power and beauty.

Designed by the legendary Las Vegas architect Steve Wynn, the Mirage Volcano was one of the first free outdoor shows on the Strip and set a new standard for entertainment in the city. The attraction underwent a significant renovation in 2008, with updates by WET Design, the creators of the Bellagio Fountains, enhancing its visual and auditory effects.

The Mirage Volcano eruptions occur nightly, typically every hour from dusk until midnight. Each eruption lasts several minutes, featuring a choreographed performance of fiery explosions, shooting flames, and cascading water set to a soundtrack composed by Grateful Dead drummer Mickey Hart and Indian tabla virtuoso Zakir Hussain. The music, combined with the dramatic visual effects, creates an immersive and thrilling experience for viewers.

The volcano is surrounded by lush landscaping, including palm trees and waterfalls, which add to the tropical ambiance of The Mirage. The use of pyrotechnics and specially designed flame jets allows the volcano to shoot fireballs more than 12 feet into the air, illuminating the night sky and reflecting off the surrounding water to create a dazzling spectacle.

The Mirage Volcano is not only a testament to Las Vegas's ability to create awe-inspiring attractions but also a tribute to the innovative spirit of the city's entertainment industry. Its blend of natural elements and cutting-edge technology continues to draw crowds and remains a must-see attraction for visitors to the Strip.

In addition to the nightly eruptions, The Mirage offers various viewing spots for the volcano show, including prime locations along Las Vegas Boulevard and from the resort's outdoor terraces. This accessibility ensures that visitors can enjoy the show from multiple vantage points, making it a memorable highlight of their Las Vegas experience.

Overall, the Mirage Volcano stands as a symbol of the city's flair for dramatic and imaginative entertainment. Its fiery eruptions and captivating performances make it a standout attraction that continues to enchant and delight audiences from around the world.

The Smith Center for the Performing Arts is a premier cultural destination in Las Vegas, offering a world-class venue for a diverse range of performances, from Broadway shows and concerts to ballet and classical music. Opened in 2012, the Smith Center is located in downtown Las Vegas's Symphony Park and has quickly established itself as the city's heart of the arts.

The Smith Center's design reflects an Art Deco aesthetic, inspired by the Hoover Dam's architectural style, and features stunning limestone facades, intricate detailing, and a grand 17-story carillon tower. The center encompasses three performance spaces: Reynolds Hall, Myron's Cabaret Jazz, and Troesh Studio Theater, each designed to provide an intimate and acoustically superior experience.

Reynolds Hall is the centerpiece of the Smith Center, with a seating capacity of over 2,000. This grand theater hosts a wide array of performances, including touring Broadway productions, symphony orchestra concerts, and renowned solo artists. The hall's state-of-the-art acoustics and elegant design make it an ideal venue for both large-scale productions and intimate performances.

Myron's Cabaret Jazz offers a more intimate setting with seating for about 240 guests. This venue is known for its cabaret-style performances, featuring jazz, blues, and contemporary music acts in a cozy, club-like atmosphere. The flexible seating arrangement and excellent acoustics provide a perfect environment for close-up performances and engaging shows.

The Troesh Studio Theater, with a capacity of around 250, is a versatile black-box space used for experimental theater, dance, and smaller-scale productions. This flexible venue allows for creative staging and diverse programming, making it a vital part of the Smith Center's mission to support emerging and innovative art forms.

In addition to its performance spaces, the Smith Center offers educational programs and community outreach initiatives aimed at fostering a love of the arts in the Las Vegas community. These programs include student matinees, masterclasses, and partnerships with local schools and organizations.

Overall, the Smith Center for the Performing Arts stands as a beacon of cultural enrichment in Las Vegas. Its dedication to providing world-class performances and fostering arts education makes it a vital and vibrant part of the city's cultural landscape.

Brooklyn Bowl Las Vegas

Brooklyn Bowl Las Vegas, located in the LINQ Promenade, is a unique entertainment venue that combines live music, gourmet dining, and bowling in an energetic and eclectic atmosphere. Opened in 2014, this venue is a branch of the original Brooklyn Bowl in New York City and has quickly become a popular destination for both locals and tourists seeking a one-of-a-kind experience on the Las Vegas Strip.

The venue spans 80,000 square feet and features a concert hall with a capacity of up to 2,000 people. The concert space hosts a diverse range of live music performances, from rock and hip-hop to electronic and indie acts. The state-of-the-art sound and lighting systems ensure that every show delivers an exceptional audio-visual experience, making it a favorite spot for music lovers.

One of the standout features of Brooklyn Bowl Las Vegas is its 32-lane bowling alley, which adds a fun and interactive element to the venue. Guests can enjoy bowling while listening to live music, creating a lively and dynamic environment that sets it apart from traditional concert halls and bowling alleys. The lanes are equipped with comfortable seating and modern amenities, making it an ideal spot for both casual bowlers and serious enthusiasts.

Brooklyn Bowl also boasts an extensive menu created by renowned restaurateur Bruce Bromberg, offering a variety of gourmet comfort foods. The menu features items like fried chicken, French bread pizzas, and house-smoked barbecue, along with a selection of craft beers and specialty cocktails. The venue's dining options are designed to complement the entertainment experience, allowing guests to enjoy delicious food and drinks while taking in a show or bowling a few frames.

In addition to its regular programming, Brooklyn Bowl Las Vegas hosts special events, private parties, and corporate functions. The versatile space can be customized to accommodate a wide range of events, making it a popular choice for celebrations and gatherings.

Overall, Brooklyn Bowl Las Vegas offers a vibrant and multifaceted entertainment experience that combines live music, dining, and bowling in a unique and engaging setting. Its eclectic atmosphere, top-notch performances, and fun amenities make it a must-visit destination on the Las Vegas Strip.

Park Theater at Park MGM

The Park Theater at Park MGM is a modern, state-of-the-art entertainment venue located on the Las Vegas Strip. Opened in 2016, this theater has quickly become a premier destination for top-tier performances, hosting an array of concerts, residencies, and special events that attract visitors from around the world.

The Park Theater is designed to offer an intimate yet grand experience, with a seating capacity of approximately 5,200. The theater's layout ensures excellent sightlines and acoustics from every seat, providing a first-class experience for all attendees. The design features a blend of contemporary aesthetics and comfort, making it an ideal venue for enjoying world-class entertainment.

One of the theater's main attractions is its impressive roster of resident artists and headliners. Over the years, the Park Theater has hosted residencies by some of the biggest names in music, including Lady Gaga, Bruno Mars, Cher, and Aerosmith. These long-term engagements allow fans to experience their favorite artists in a more personal and exclusive setting compared to larger arena tours.

The Park Theater is equipped with cutting-edge technology, including high-definition video screens, advanced lighting systems, and a powerful sound system. These features enhance the overall performance, creating an immersive and visually stunning experience for the audience. The theater's technical capabilities also allow for elaborate stage productions and dynamic show designs, making it a versatile space for various types of performances.

In addition to its concert offerings, the Park Theater hosts a variety of special events, including comedy shows, award ceremonies, and corporate functions. The venue's flexible seating arrangements and modern amenities make it suitable for a wide range of events, catering to diverse audiences.

The Park Theater is part of the larger Park MGM resort, which offers an array of dining, shopping, and entertainment options. Visitors can enjoy a meal at one of the resort's acclaimed restaurants, such as Bavette's Steakhouse & Bar or Eataly, before heading to the theater for a show. The proximity to The Park, an outdoor dining and entertainment district, further enhances the overall experience, providing a lively and dynamic atmosphere.

Overall, the Park Theater at Park MGM stands out as one of the top entertainment venues on the Las Vegas Strip. Its combination of world-class performances, modern amenities, and intimate setting make it a must-visit destination for anyone seeking top-tier entertainment in Las Vegas.

House of Blues

The House of Blues Las Vegas, located inside the Mandalay Bay Resort and Casino, is a premier entertainment venue known for its eclectic lineup of live music, vibrant atmosphere, and Southern-inspired cuisine. Since opening its doors in 1999, the House of Blues has become a beloved destination for both locals and tourists seeking an authentic and energetic concert experience on the Las Vegas Strip.

The House of Blues is designed to reflect the rich cultural heritage of the American South, with a unique decor that features folk art, eclectic murals, and various blues memorabilia. This warm and inviting ambiance creates a distinctive setting that enhances the overall concert experience. The venue can accommodate up to 1,800 guests, providing an intimate atmosphere that allows for close interaction between the performers and the audience.

The music lineup at the House of Blues is diverse, featuring a wide range of genres, including rock, blues, jazz, hip-hop, and country. The venue is known for hosting both established artists and emerging talent, ensuring a dynamic and ever-changing roster of performances. In addition to concerts, the House of Blues also offers special events such as gospel brunches, where guests can enjoy a delicious Southern-style buffet while listening to live gospel music.

One of the standout features of the House of Blues Las Vegas is its Foundation Room, an exclusive members-only club located on the top floor of Mandalay Bay. The Foundation Room offers stunning views of the Las Vegas skyline, luxurious decor, and a sophisticated atmosphere. Members and guests can enjoy upscale dining, handcrafted cocktails, and private events in this elegant space.

The House of Blues is also renowned for its Southern-inspired cuisine, which can be enjoyed in the concert hall or the adjacent restaurant. The menu features classic dishes such as jambalaya, gumbo, fried catfish, and barbecue ribs, all prepared with a contemporary twist. The combination of great music, delicious food, and a lively atmosphere makes the House of Blues a must-visit destination for entertainment in Las Vegas.

Overall, the House of Blues Las Vegas offers a unique and memorable concert experience that blends music, art, and culture. Its commitment to showcasing a diverse range of talent and providing top-notch hospitality makes it a standout venue on the Las Vegas entertainment scene.

The Joint at Hard Rock

The Joint at Hard Rock, now known as The Joint at Virgin Hotels Las Vegas, is a legendary concert venue renowned for its intimate setting, exceptional acoustics, and star-studded lineup of performances. Originally opened in 1995 as part of the Hard Rock Hotel & Casino, The Joint quickly established itself as one of the top live music venues in Las Vegas. Following the hotel's rebranding to Virgin Hotels in 2020, The Joint continues to be a premier destination for live entertainment.

The Joint is designed to provide an unparalleled concert experience, with a seating capacity of approximately 4,000. The venue's layout ensures excellent sightlines and acoustics from every seat, making it a favorite among both performers and audiences. The combination of a state-of-the-art sound system, advanced lighting, and intimate atmosphere creates an immersive and memorable experience for concertgoers.

Over the years, The Joint has hosted an impressive array of artists and bands from various genres, including rock, pop, hip-hop, and country. Legendary performers such as The Rolling Stones, Paul McCartney, Guns N' Roses, and Aerosmith have graced its stage, solidifying The Joint's reputation as a premier venue for live music. The venue is also known for its high-energy residencies, featuring acts like Def Leppard, Journey, and Imagine Dragons.

In addition to concerts, The Joint hosts a variety of other events, including comedy shows, award ceremonies, and special events. Its versatile design and modern amenities make it an ideal venue for a wide range of performances and gatherings.

The Joint is part of the vibrant Virgin Hotels Las Vegas, which offers a variety of dining, entertainment, and nightlife options. Visitors can enjoy a meal at one of the hotel's acclaimed restaurants, such as Nobu or One Steakhouse, before heading to The Joint for a show. The hotel's lively casino, luxurious accommodations, and stylish decor further enhance the overall experience, providing a complete entertainment package.

Overall, The Joint at Virgin Hotels Las Vegas continues to be a premier live music venue, known for its exceptional acoustics, intimate setting, and diverse lineup of performances. Its commitment to providing top-tier entertainment and unforgettable experiences makes it a must-visit destination for music lovers in Las Vegas.

Planet Hollywood Theater

The Planet Hollywood Theater, also known as the Zappos Theater, is a state-of-the-art entertainment venue located within the Planet Hollywood Resort & Casino on the Las Vegas Strip. Renowned for its impressive lineup of resident shows, concerts, and special events, the theater offers a premier entertainment experience in the heart of Las Vegas.

With a seating capacity of approximately 7,000, the Planet Hollywood Theater is one of the largest indoor theaters on the Strip. The venue's design ensures excellent sightlines and acoustics from every seat, providing an immersive and engaging experience for all attendees. The theater is equipped with advanced sound and lighting systems, as well as high-definition video screens, enhancing the visual and auditory elements of each performance.

The Planet Hollywood Theater is famous for its residency shows, featuring some of the biggest names in music and entertainment. Over the years, the venue has hosted iconic performers such as Britney Spears, Jennifer Lopez, Pitbull, Gwen Stefani, and Christina Aguilera. These long-term engagements offer fans a unique opportunity to see their favorite artists in an intimate and high-energy setting.

In addition to its resident shows, the theater hosts a variety of concerts, comedy acts, and special events throughout the year. The diverse programming ensures that there is always something exciting happening at the venue, catering to a wide range of tastes and preferences.

The theater's location within the Planet Hollywood Resort & Casino adds to its appeal, offering visitors easy access to a variety of dining, shopping, and entertainment options. The resort features numerous restaurants, including celebrity chef establishments like Gordon Ramsay Burger and Koi, providing guests with a range of culinary experiences. The Miracle Mile Shops, an extensive retail complex, offers a diverse selection of stores and boutiques, making it a perfect destination for shopping enthusiasts.

The Planet Hollywood Theater's combination of world-class entertainment, modern amenities, and convenient location makes it a standout venue on the Las Vegas Strip. Whether you're attending a concert, a comedy show, or a residency performance, the theater provides an unforgettable experience that captures the excitement and glamour of Las Vegas.

Overall, the Planet Hollywood Theater is a premier entertainment destination, known for its impressive lineup of performances and top-tier facilities. Its commitment to providing high-quality shows and memorable experiences makes it a must-visit venue for anyone seeking the best of Las Vegas entertainment.

Historic Sites

Old Las Vegas Mormon Fort State Historic Park

Old Las Vegas Mormon Fort State Historic Park is a historic site in downtown Las Vegas that offers a glimpse into the early history of the city. Established in 1855, the fort was built by Mormon missionaries and is considered the first permanent non-native settlement in the Las Vegas Valley. The park preserves this important historical site and educates visitors about the area's early history and development.

The fort was initially constructed as a way station for travelers on the Old Spanish Trail and as a missionary outpost. The original adobe structure included living quarters, a blacksmith shop, and other essential facilities. Although the Mormon mission was abandoned after only two years, the fort continued to serve as a key location for travelers, traders, and settlers in the region.

Today, visitors to the Old Las Vegas Mormon Fort State Historic Park can explore the reconstructed fort and see remnants of the original structure. The park features a visitor center with exhibits detailing the history of the fort, the missionaries who built it, and its significance in the development of Las Vegas. Artifacts, photographs, and interactive displays provide a comprehensive overview of the site's historical importance.

The park also hosts various educational programs and events throughout the year, including living history demonstrations, guided tours, and workshops. These activities offer visitors a hands-on opportunity to learn about the daily lives of the fort's inhabitants and the challenges they faced.

The surrounding grounds of the park include picnic areas and walking trails, providing a peaceful setting for visitors to enjoy the natural beauty of the area. The park's location in the heart of Las Vegas makes it an easily accessible destination for both locals and tourists.

Overall, Old Las Vegas Mormon Fort State Historic Park is a significant historical site that offers a unique perspective on the early history of Las Vegas. Its well-preserved structures, informative exhibits, and engaging programs make it a must-visit destination for anyone interested in the origins and development of the city.

Springs Preserve is a 180-acre cultural and historical attraction located just a few miles from the Las Vegas Strip. Dedicated to preserving the natural and cultural heritage of the Las Vegas Valley, Springs Preserve offers a variety of exhibits, interactive displays, and outdoor experiences that showcase the region's rich history, ecology, and sustainability efforts.

One of the main highlights of Springs Preserve is the Origen Museum, which features exhibits on the history of the Las Vegas Valley, from its prehistoric origins to its modern development. The museum's interactive displays and multimedia presentations provide an engaging and educational experience for visitors of all ages. Exhibits cover topics such as the geology of the area, the early Native American inhabitants, and the arrival of European settlers.

The Nevada State Museum, Las Vegas, is also located within Springs Preserve. This museum offers a deeper dive into the state's history, with exhibits on topics like mining, the construction of the Hoover Dam, and the development of Las Vegas as a major tourist destination.

Springs Preserve is home to several beautifully landscaped botanical gardens, showcasing a variety of desert plants and sustainable gardening practices. The gardens serve as both an educational resource and a peaceful retreat, allowing visitors to explore the diverse flora of the Mojave Desert. The Desert Living Center, located within the gardens, provides information on sustainable living and conservation efforts, promoting environmental awareness and stewardship.

For outdoor enthusiasts, Springs Preserve offers miles of trails that wind through the desert landscape, providing opportunities for hiking, biking, and wildlife viewing. The trails are designed to highlight the natural beauty of the area and include interpretive signs that educate visitors about the local ecosystem and its inhabitants.

Springs Preserve also hosts a variety of events and educational programs throughout the year, including workshops, guided tours, and seasonal festivals. These activities aim to foster a deeper understanding and appreciation of the region's natural and cultural heritage.

Overall, Springs Preserve is a unique and multifaceted attraction that offers a comprehensive look at the history, ecology, and sustainability efforts of the Las Vegas Valley. Its blend of educational exhibits, beautiful gardens, and outdoor activities make it a must-visit destination for anyone looking to explore the natural and cultural richness of the area.

The Hoover Dam Bypass, officially known as the Mike O'Callaghan-Pat Tillman Memorial Bridge, is a remarkable engineering feat that enhances the iconic Hoover Dam experience. Completed in 2010, the bypass bridge spans the Colorado River and connects the states of Nevada and Arizona, providing a crucial transportation link while offering breathtaking views of the dam and the surrounding landscape.

Named in honor of Mike O'Callaghan, a former Nevada governor, and Pat Tillman, an NFL player and Army Ranger who was killed in Afghanistan, the bridge stands as a tribute to their legacies. The Hoover Dam Bypass was constructed to alleviate traffic congestion on the narrow and winding road that previously traversed the top of the dam. This new route not only improves safety and efficiency for motorists but also preserves the integrity and tranquility of the dam for visitors.

The bridge is an impressive structure, measuring 1,900 feet in length and towering 900 feet above the Colorado River. It is the longest single-span concrete arch bridge in North America and one of the highest bridges in the world. The bridge's sleek, modern design complements the timeless elegance of the Hoover Dam, creating a striking visual contrast.

Visitors to the Hoover Dam Bypass can access a pedestrian walkway that runs alongside the bridge, offering unparalleled views of the dam, the Colorado River, and the surrounding Black Canyon. The walkway is equipped with informational plaques that provide insights into the bridge's construction and the history of the Hoover Dam, enriching the visitor experience.

The bridge is part of the larger Hoover Dam Visitor Center complex, which includes exhibits, tours, and educational programs about the dam's construction, its impact on the region, and its role in American history. The visitor center offers guided tours that take guests inside the dam, providing a close-up look at its massive infrastructure and the powerful turbines that generate hydroelectric power.

Overall, the Hoover Dam Bypass enhances the visitor experience by offering stunning vistas and improving access to one of America's most iconic landmarks. Its engineering excellence and scenic beauty make it a must-visit destination for anyone traveling to the Hoover Dam.

Clark County Museum

The Clark County Museum, located in Henderson, Nevada, offers a comprehensive look at the history and cultural heritage of the Las Vegas Valley and the surrounding region. Spanning 30 acres, the museum features a variety of exhibits, historical buildings, and artifacts that tell the story of Southern Nevada's development from prehistoric times to the present.

One of the highlights of the Clark County Museum is Heritage Street, a collection of restored historic buildings that provide a glimpse into the everyday life of Southern Nevada residents throughout the decades. Visitors can explore a range of structures, including a 1912 railroad cottage, a 1930s-era church, and a 1950s mid-century modern house. Each building is furnished with period-appropriate decor and artifacts, offering an immersive experience that brings history to life.

The museum's indoor exhibit hall, the Anna Roberts Parks Exhibit Hall, features a wide array of displays covering various aspects of regional history. Exhibits include Native American artifacts, mining tools, vintage gaming devices, and memorabilia from the early days of Las Vegas. The hall also showcases rotating exhibits that delve into specific themes or events in the area's history, providing fresh and engaging content for repeat visitors.

The Clark County Museum also highlights the natural history of the region, with exhibits on the geology, flora, and fauna of the Mojave Desert. Visitors can learn about the unique ecosystems and wildlife that inhabit the area, as well as the environmental challenges and conservation efforts that impact Southern Nevada.

In addition to its exhibits, the museum offers a range of educational programs and events designed to engage the community and promote an understanding of local history. These include guided tours, workshops, lectures, and special events such as heritage days and craft fairs. The museum's staff and volunteers are dedicated to preserving and sharing the rich history of Clark County, making it a valuable resource for both residents and tourists.

The Clark County Museum's extensive grounds also feature picnic areas, walking paths, and outdoor exhibits, providing a pleasant and informative environment for visitors to explore at their own pace.

Overall, the Clark County Museum offers a fascinating and comprehensive look at the history and culture of Southern Nevada. Its diverse exhibits, historical buildings, and engaging programs make it a must-visit destination for anyone interested in the rich heritage of the Las Vegas Valley.

Boulder City Historic District

Boulder City Historic District, located just a short drive from Las Vegas, offers a charming glimpse into the history of one of Nevada's most significant towns. Established in the early 1930s to house workers building the Hoover Dam, Boulder City retains much of its small-town charm and historic character, making it a popular destination for those interested in the region's past.

The district is home to a variety of well-preserved buildings and sites that reflect its origins as a company town. Key attractions include the Boulder Dam Hotel, built in 1933, which now houses the Boulder City/Hoover Dam Museum. This museum provides a fascinating overview of the town's history, the construction of the Hoover Dam, and the lives of the workers who built it. Exhibits include photographs, artifacts, and personal stories that bring this pivotal period to life.

Another notable site in the historic district is the Boulder Theatre, an Art Deco building from 1931 that originally served as a cinema for dam workers and their families. Today, the theatre hosts a variety of performances and events, preserving its role as a cultural hub for the community.

Visitors can also explore several historic homes and buildings that have been converted into shops, restaurants, and galleries, adding to the district's vibrant atmosphere. The pedestrian-friendly streets are lined with quaint boutiques, antique stores, and cafes, making it a pleasant area to stroll and shop.

The Boulder City Historic District regularly hosts events and festivals that celebrate the town's heritage and community spirit. The annual Boulder City Art Guild's Spring Jamboree and the Boulder City Winter Art Fest are just a few examples of the cultural events that attract visitors throughout the year.

Overall, Boulder City Historic District offers a unique blend of history, culture, and small-town charm. Its well-preserved architecture, engaging museums, and lively community events make it a must-visit destination for anyone interested in the history of the Hoover Dam and the development of Southern Nevada.

Las Vegas Pioneer Trail

The Las Vegas Pioneer Trail is a self-guided tour that takes visitors through some of the most historically significant sites in Las Vegas. Developed to showcase the rich and diverse history of the area, the trail features a series of markers and informational plaques that provide insights into the early development of the city and its surrounding region.

The trail includes several notable landmarks that reflect Las Vegas's transformation from a small desert settlement to a bustling metropolis. One of the key sites on the trail is the Old Las Vegas Mormon Fort State Historic Park, the first permanent non-native settlement in the Las Vegas Valley. This site offers a glimpse into the early days of Las Vegas, with reconstructed buildings and exhibits detailing the lives of the Mormon missionaries who established the fort in 1855.

Another important stop on the Pioneer Trail is the Historic Fifth Street School, built in 1936. This building served as a key educational institution during Las Vegas's early years and has been restored to preserve its original architectural features. Today, it functions as a cultural center, hosting art exhibitions, performances, and community events.

The trail also includes several historic homes and buildings that illustrate the development of Las Vegas over the decades. The Harrison House, for example, was a significant site during the Civil Rights Movement, providing lodging for African American entertainers who were not allowed to stay in the major hotels on the Strip. The trail highlights the cultural and social changes that have shaped the city's history.

Other notable sites on the Las Vegas Pioneer Trail include the Las Vegas Springs Preserve, which explores the natural history of the region and the vital role of water in the city's development, and the Morelli House, a mid-century modern home that exemplifies the architectural style of 1950s Las Vegas.

Overall, the Las Vegas Pioneer Trail offers a comprehensive and engaging way to explore the city's rich history. By following the trail, visitors can gain a deeper understanding of the people, events, and developments that have contributed to the unique character of Las Vegas.

Tule Springs Fossil Beds National Monument, located in the northern part of the Las Vegas Valley, is a significant paleontological site that offers a unique glimpse into the prehistoric past of the region. Established as a national monument in 2014, Tule Springs preserves a rich array of fossils that date back to the Ice Age, providing valuable insights into the ancient ecosystems that once thrived in this area.

The monument spans approximately 22,650 acres and is renowned for its well-preserved fossils of large Pleistocene-era animals. Among the most notable finds are the remains of mammoths, horses, camels, bison, and saber-toothed cats. These fossils are critical for understanding the environmental changes and biodiversity of the region during the last Ice Age, around 200,000 to 10,000 years ago.

Visitors to Tule Springs Fossil Beds National Monument can explore the landscape and see the fossil beds that have yielded these remarkable discoveries. While the monument does not currently have a visitor center, informational signs and designated trails provide context and guidance for those exploring the area. The terrain features expansive desert vistas, dry lake beds, and significant geological formations that add to the site's scientific and scenic value.

The monument is also an important area for ongoing scientific research. Paleontologists and geologists conduct field studies to uncover new fossils and gain further understanding of the region's ancient past. Public events and volunteer opportunities occasionally allow visitors to participate in digs and learn more about the science of paleontology.

In addition to its paleontological significance, Tule Springs Fossil Beds National Monument offers a habitat for modern wildlife and native plants. The area is home to a variety of desert species, including jackrabbits, coyotes, and numerous bird species. Visitors can enjoy birdwatching and wildlife viewing as they explore the monument.

Overall, Tule Springs Fossil Beds National Monument provides a fascinating journey into the prehistoric world of Southern Nevada. Its extensive fossil record, scientific importance, and natural beauty make it a compelling destination for anyone interested in paleontology, geology, and the history of life on Earth.

Harrison House

Harrison House is a significant historic site in Las Vegas, known for its crucial role during the Civil Rights Movement. Located in the Westside neighborhood, this modest house served as a haven for African American entertainers and other notable figures who visited Las Vegas during the mid-20th century. Built in 1942, Harrison House was one of the few places where African Americans could find lodging due to the segregation policies that prevailed at the time.

The house was owned by Genevieve Harrison, an African American woman who opened her doors to prominent black entertainers who were performing on the Las Vegas Strip but were not allowed to stay in the hotels where they performed. Notable guests included legendary performers such as Nat King Cole, Sammy Davis Jr., and Lena Horne. Harrison House became a cultural hub and a symbol of resistance against the racial segregation that was pervasive in Las Vegas during that era.

Today, Harrison House stands as a testament to the struggles and triumphs of the African American community in Las Vegas. Efforts have been made to preserve the house and its history, and it has been recognized as an important cultural and historical landmark. Visitors can tour the house and learn about its significance through exhibits and educational programs that highlight the stories of the entertainers who stayed there and the broader context of the Civil Rights Movement in Las Vegas.

The house's preservation serves as a reminder of the progress that has been made in the fight for equality and the importance of remembering and honoring those who paved the way. Harrison House is not just a building; it is a symbol of community, resilience, and the enduring legacy of those who fought for civil rights in Las Vegas and beyond.

Little Church of the West

The Little Church of the West is a historic wedding chapel located on the Las Vegas Strip. Established in 1942, it is one of the oldest buildings on the Strip and has become an iconic symbol of Las Vegas's reputation as the wedding capital of the world. Designed to resemble a picturesque pioneer church, the Little Church of the West has hosted thousands of weddings, including those of many celebrities.

The chapel's charming design features rustic wooden architecture, stained glass windows, and a quaint steeple, creating a romantic and intimate setting for wedding ceremonies. The interior is equally enchanting, with wooden pews, a cozy altar, and a warm ambiance that makes it a perfect venue for couples seeking a classic and timeless wedding experience.

The Little Church of the West has a rich history and has been listed on the National Register of Historic Places. Over the years, it has been the site of numerous high-profile weddings, including those of celebrities such as Judy Garland, Richard Gere, Cindy Crawford, and Angelina Jolie. Its legacy as a preferred wedding destination for both famous and ordinary couples adds to its allure and charm.

In addition to weddings, the chapel offers vow renewals and commitment ceremonies, accommodating a wide range of romantic celebrations. The Little Church of the West provides various wedding packages that include photography, floral arrangements, limousine service, and personalized ceremonies, ensuring a memorable and stress-free experience for couples.

The chapel's convenient location on the Strip makes it easily accessible for both locals and tourists. Its proximity to major hotels, casinos, and entertainment venues allows couples to seamlessly integrate their wedding festivities with the vibrant energy of Las Vegas.

The Little Church of the West continues to uphold its tradition of providing beautiful and meaningful wedding ceremonies. Its historic significance, picturesque setting, and reputation for excellence make it a standout choice for couples looking to tie the knot in Las Vegas. Whether for a grand celebration or an intimate elopement, the Little Church of the West offers a timeless and romantic venue for creating lasting memories.

Old Las Vegas Mormon Fort State Historic Park

The Old Las Vegas Mormon Fort State Historic Park is a significant historical site that offers a glimpse into the early history of Las Vegas and the broader story of western expansion in the United States. Established in 1855 by a group of 30 Mormon missionaries, the fort was the first permanent non-native settlement in the Las Vegas Valley. The missionaries were sent by Brigham Young, the leader of the Church of Jesus Christ of Latter-day Saints (LDS), to establish an outpost that would serve as a way station for travelers between Salt Lake City and the Pacific Coast.

The fort, built from adobe bricks, was strategically located near a natural spring, which provided a reliable source of water in the arid desert environment. This water source, known as the Las Vegas Springs, was crucial not only for the survival of the settlers but also for the many travelers who passed through the area. The fort quickly became a vital stop on the Old Spanish Trail, offering supplies, shelter, and protection in what was then a remote and challenging landscape.

Although the Mormon missionaries abandoned the fort in 1857 due to difficulties with the local environment and conflicts with Native American tribes, the site continued to play a role in the development of Las Vegas. It later served as a ranch, and the area around it eventually grew into the bustling city we know today.

Today, the Old Las Vegas Mormon Fort is preserved as a state historic park, where visitors can explore the remains of the original adobe structure and learn about the early settlers through exhibits and interpretive displays. The visitor center offers detailed insights into the fort's history, including the daily lives of the missionaries, their interactions with Native American tribes, and the challenges they faced in the harsh desert environment.

The park provides a fascinating window into a lesser-known chapter of Las Vegas history, showcasing the determination and resilience of the early pioneers who laid the groundwork for the city's future growth.

Observation Decks

Stratosphere Tower Observation Deck

The Stratosphere Tower Observation Deck, located at The STRAT Hotel, Casino & SkyPod, is one of the most iconic and thrilling attractions in Las Vegas. Standing at an impressive 1,149 feet, it is the tallest freestanding observation tower in the United States and offers unparalleled panoramic views of the Las Vegas Strip, the surrounding desert landscape, and the distant mountains.

The observation deck is divided into two levels: the indoor deck on Level 108 and the outdoor deck on Level 109. The indoor deck is enclosed with floor-to-ceiling glass windows, providing a comfortable and climate-controlled environment where visitors can take in the stunning vistas. Interactive displays and high-powered telescopes enhance the experience, allowing guests to pinpoint and learn about various landmarks.

For those seeking an adrenaline rush, the outdoor deck offers an exhilarating open-air experience. It features glass barriers for safety while providing an unobstructed 360-degree view of the city. The fresh air and height combine to create a thrilling sensation that is hard to match.

In addition to the breathtaking views, the Stratosphere Tower Observation Deck is home to several heart-pounding attractions. SkyJump Las Vegas is a controlled free-fall experience that lets thrill-seekers jump off the tower and descend 855 feet at speeds of up to 40 mph. The Big Shot catapults riders 160 feet in the air from the top of the tower, offering a brief moment of weightlessness. Insanity is a mechanical arm that extends over the edge of the tower and spins riders at high speeds, providing a dizzying view of the ground far below.

The tower also boasts a revolving restaurant, Top of the World, which completes a full rotation every 80 minutes, allowing diners to enjoy a gourmet meal while taking in the ever-changing view. For a more casual experience, the 107 SkyLounge offers cocktails and light bites with spectacular views.

Overall, the Stratosphere Tower Observation Deck is a must-visit destination for anyone looking to experience Las Vegas from a new perspective. Its combination of stunning views, thrilling attractions, and unique dining options make it a standout highlight of the city.

The High Roller at The LINQ is an iconic attraction on the Las Vegas Strip, offering a unique and exhilarating way to take in the city's famous skyline. Opened in 2014, the High Roller is the world's tallest observation wheel, standing at an impressive 550 feet. Located at The LINQ Promenade, a bustling outdoor shopping, dining, and entertainment district, the High Roller has quickly become a must-visit destination for both tourists and locals.

The High Roller features 28 spacious, air-conditioned cabins, each capable of holding up to 40 passengers. These cabins are equipped with large windows that provide a 360-degree view of Las Vegas and the surrounding landscape. The ride takes approximately 30 minutes to complete one full rotation, offering ample time for passengers to enjoy the breathtaking vistas and capture stunning photographs.

One of the highlights of the High Roller experience is the variety of cabin options available. In addition to standard cabins, the High Roller offers Happy Half Hour cabins, which include an open bar and a bartender, allowing passengers to enjoy cocktails while taking in the view. This option adds a festive and social element to the ride, making it perfect for celebrations and group outings.

The views from the High Roller are spectacular at any time of day, but nighttime rides are particularly popular due to the dazzling lights of the Las Vegas Strip. The wheel itself is illuminated with colorful LED lights, which change in synchronization with music and special events, creating a vibrant and dynamic display that enhances the overall experience.

The High Roller is more than just an observation wheel; it's part of the larger LINQ Promenade experience. Visitors can explore a variety of shops, restaurants, and entertainment venues before or after their ride. Popular dining options include Gordon Ramsay Fish & Chips, Yard House, and Chayo Mexican Kitchen + Tequila Bar. The promenade also features attractions like the FLY LINQ Zipline and virtual reality experiences, providing a full day of entertainment.

Overall, the High Roller at The LINQ offers a unique and memorable way to see Las Vegas from above. Its impressive height, comfortable cabins, and spectacular views make it a standout attraction that provides a fresh perspective on the city's famous skyline.

The Eiffel Tower Viewing Deck at Paris Las Vegas brings a slice of Parisian elegance to the heart of the Las Vegas Strip. This half-scale replica of the iconic Eiffel Tower stands at 541 feet and offers stunning panoramic views of the city, making it one of the most popular attractions in Las Vegas. Opened in 1999, the Eiffel Tower Viewing Deck combines romantic ambiance with breathtaking vistas, providing a unique experience that transports visitors to the City of Light.

Visitors begin their journey by taking a glass elevator ride up to the observation deck, which is located 46 stories above the Strip. The ride itself is a thrilling ascent that offers glimpses of the Las Vegas skyline as you rise. Once at the top, the observation deck provides a 360-degree view of the surrounding area, including the vibrant lights of the Strip, the distant mountains, and iconic landmarks such as the Bellagio Fountains, which can be seen in their full glory from this vantage point.

The Eiffel Tower Viewing Deck is particularly popular at night when the city is illuminated with neon lights, creating a magical and romantic atmosphere. The deck is open until late, allowing visitors to take in the beauty of Las Vegas under the stars. Knowledgeable staff are on hand to point out landmarks and provide interesting facts about the city and the tower itself.

In addition to the viewing deck, the Eiffel Tower at Paris Las Vegas features the Eiffel Tower Restaurant, located halfway up the structure. This fine dining establishment offers gourmet French cuisine and stunning views, making it an ideal spot for a special dinner or celebration. The combination of exquisite food and breathtaking scenery creates an unforgettable dining experience.

The Eiffel Tower Viewing Deck also hosts various events and special occasions, such as marriage proposals and wedding ceremonies, adding a touch of Parisian romance to these memorable moments. The tower's unique setting and panoramic views make it a favorite spot for couples looking to create lasting memories.

Overall, the Eiffel Tower Viewing Deck at Paris Las Vegas offers a unique blend of elegance, romance, and stunning vistas. Its combination of architectural beauty, exceptional views, and Parisian charm makes it a must-visit destination for anyone looking to experience the allure of Las Vegas from a new perspective.

Skyfall Lounge, located on the 64th floor of the Delano Las Vegas, is a sophisticated and stylish rooftop bar offering stunning panoramic views of the Las Vegas Strip and the surrounding desert landscape. Opened in 2014, this upscale lounge combines a chic atmosphere with expertly crafted cocktails, making it a popular destination for both locals and tourists seeking a memorable night out.

The design of Skyfall Lounge is modern and elegant, featuring sleek furnishings, ambient lighting, and floor-to-ceiling windows that provide unobstructed views of the city. The spacious outdoor terrace is a highlight, offering a comfortable and inviting space where guests can relax and take in the breathtaking scenery. The terrace is equipped with plush seating and heaters, ensuring a pleasant experience regardless of the season.

Skyfall Lounge is renowned for its innovative cocktail menu, created by skilled mixologists who use premium spirits and fresh ingredients to craft unique and delicious drinks. Signature cocktails include the "Skyfall," a refreshing blend of vodka, elderflower liqueur, and lemon, and the "Desert Sunset," a vibrant mix of tequila, blood orange, and agave. The lounge also offers an extensive selection of wines, champagnes, and craft beers, catering to a wide range of tastes.

In addition to its impressive drink offerings, Skyfall Lounge features a menu of gourmet small plates and appetizers, perfect for sharing and pairing with cocktails. Dishes include truffle fries, sliders, and artisanal cheese boards, providing a delightful culinary complement to the drinks and views.

Skyfall Lounge is also known for its lively and energetic atmosphere, with resident DJs spinning a mix of contemporary and classic tracks that keep the vibe upbeat and engaging. The lounge often hosts special events and themed nights, adding an extra layer of excitement to the experience.

Overall, Skyfall Lounge at Delano offers a sophisticated and stylish setting for enjoying cocktails and taking in the stunning views of Las Vegas. Its combination of elegant design, exceptional drinks, and vibrant atmosphere make it a must-visit destination for anyone looking to experience the best of the city's nightlife.

The Foundation Room at Mandalay Bay is a luxurious rooftop lounge and nightclub offering an exclusive and elegant nightlife experience. Located on the 63rd floor of the Mandalay Bay Resort and Casino, the Foundation Room provides breathtaking views of the Las Vegas Strip and an opulent setting that combines sophistication with a touch of mystique.

The decor of the Foundation Room is inspired by exotic and eclectic styles, featuring rich fabrics, intricate woodwork, and an array of unique artifacts and artwork from around the world. The lounge is divided into several intimate spaces, including private rooms and secluded nooks, each adorned with its own distinctive design elements. This creates a sense of exclusivity and privacy, making it an ideal spot for intimate gatherings and special occasions.

One of the main attractions of the Foundation Room is its expansive outdoor terrace, which offers unparalleled views of the Strip's dazzling lights and iconic landmarks. The terrace is furnished with comfortable seating and ambient lighting, providing a perfect backdrop for enjoying cocktails and socializing under the stars.

The Foundation Room is renowned for its extensive menu of craft cocktails, fine wines, and premium spirits. The lounge's skilled mixologists create a variety of innovative and delicious drinks, using high-quality ingredients and creative techniques. Signature cocktails include the "Sin City Sunrise," a vibrant mix of tequila, orange liqueur, and grenadine, and the "Zen Garden," a refreshing blend of gin, cucumber, and basil. The wine list features an impressive selection of bottles from renowned vineyards, ensuring that there is something to suit every palate.

In addition to its exceptional drink offerings, the Foundation Room also boasts a menu of gourmet small plates and appetizers, crafted by talented chefs to complement the cocktails. Dishes include truffle mac and cheese, lobster flatbread, and wagyu beef sliders, providing a delectable culinary experience.

The Foundation Room hosts a variety of special events and themed nights, featuring live music, DJs, and entertainment that keep the atmosphere lively and engaging. The lounge's exclusive vibe and stunning views make it a popular destination for celebrities, VIPs, and discerning guests seeking a unique and unforgettable nightlife experience.

Overall, the Foundation Room at Mandalay Bay offers an opulent and sophisticated setting for enjoying cocktails, gourmet food, and stunning views of Las Vegas. Its combination of luxurious decor, exceptional service, and vibrant atmosphere make it a standout destination on the Strip.

VooDoo Lounge at Rio

VooDoo Lounge at Rio All-Suite Hotel & Casino is a dynamic and exciting nightlife destination known for its stunning views, vibrant atmosphere, and creative cocktails. Located on the 51st floor of the Rio, the VooDoo Lounge offers a rooftop experience that combines high-energy entertainment with breathtaking panoramas of the Las Vegas Strip and the surrounding valley.

The lounge's design is both modern and eclectic, featuring bold colors, stylish furnishings, and atmospheric lighting that create a lively and inviting ambiance. The expansive outdoor terrace is a highlight, providing an open-air space where guests can dance, socialize, and enjoy the spectacular views. The terrace is equipped with comfortable seating and fire pits, making it a perfect spot for relaxing and taking in the scenery.

VooDoo Lounge is renowned for its innovative and visually stunning cocktails, crafted by skilled mixologists who use a variety of premium spirits, fresh ingredients, and creative techniques. Signature drinks include the "Witch Doctor," a tropical concoction served in a large goblet and topped with dry ice for a dramatic smoking effect, and the "Love Potion," a fruity blend served in a test tube for a playful presentation. The lounge also offers an extensive selection of wines, beers, and other spirits, catering to a wide range of tastes.

In addition to its impressive drink offerings, VooDoo Lounge features a menu of delicious small plates and appetizers, perfect for sharing and pairing with cocktails. Dishes include shrimp skewers, mini burgers, and flatbreads, providing a tasty complement to the drinks and the vibrant atmosphere.

The entertainment at VooDoo Lounge is another major draw, with live DJs spinning a mix of popular hits, dance tracks, and classic tunes that keep the energy high and the dance floor packed. The lounge often hosts special events, themed parties, and guest performances, adding to the excitement and ensuring that there is always something new and engaging happening.

VooDoo Lounge also offers VIP packages and bottle service, providing an elevated experience for guests looking to celebrate special occasions or simply enjoy a more exclusive night out. The combination of personalized service, prime seating, and premium drinks makes it a popular choice for parties and celebrations.

Overall, VooDoo Lounge at Rio offers a dynamic and unforgettable nightlife experience that combines stunning views, innovative cocktails, and high-energy entertainment. Its vibrant atmosphere, unique drinks, and panoramic vistas make it a must-visit destination for anyone looking to experience the best of Las Vegas nightlife.

Nature and Outdoor Attractions

Lake Mead National Recreation Area

Lake Mead National Recreation Area, located just a short drive from Las Vegas, is a sprawling natural playground that offers a wide range of outdoor activities amidst stunning desert landscapes. Covering nearly 1.5 million acres, this area encompasses the vast Lake Mead and Lake Mohave, both of which were created by the damming of the Colorado River. Established in 1964, Lake Mead National Recreation Area is managed by the National Park Service and is a haven for outdoor enthusiasts.

One of the primary attractions of the area is the extensive water-based recreation available on Lake Mead and Lake Mohave. Boating, kayaking, water skiing, and fishing are popular activities, with numerous marinas and launch points providing easy access to the water. The lakes are teeming with fish, including striped bass, largemouth bass, and catfish, making them prime destinations for anglers.

In addition to water sports, the surrounding landscape offers a plethora of land-based activities. Hiking trails of varying difficulty wind through the dramatic desert scenery, featuring rugged mountains, colorful rock formations, and hidden canyons. Popular hikes include the Historic Railroad Trail, which offers spectacular views of Lake Mead and passes through old railway tunnels, and the River Mountains Loop Trail, a 34-mile multi-use trail perfect for hiking, biking, and horseback riding.

Camping is another favorite activity in Lake Mead National Recreation Area, with numerous campgrounds and RV parks available. These sites offer a chance to experience the tranquility of the desert under the starlit sky, away from the hustle and bustle of Las Vegas.

Wildlife viewing is also a draw, with the area home to diverse species such as bighorn sheep, coyotes, and a variety of birds. The stark beauty of the desert flora, including Joshua trees, creosote bushes, and blooming wildflowers, adds to the appeal.

The area also has historical significance, with sites such as the Hoover Dam Visitor Center offering insights into the monumental construction of the dam and its impact on the region.

Overall, Lake Mead National Recreation Area provides a vast array of recreational opportunities set against the backdrop of stunning desert landscapes. Whether you're seeking adventure on the water, a serene hike, or a night under the stars, this area offers something for everyone.

Valley of Fire State Park

Valley of Fire State Park, located approximately 50 miles northeast of Las Vegas, is Nevada's oldest and largest state park. Renowned for its stunning red sandstone formations, ancient petroglyphs, and vibrant desert landscapes, Valley of Fire offers a dramatic and captivating natural experience for visitors. The park spans over 40,000 acres and gets its name from the fiery red sandstone formations that appear to blaze under the sun's rays.

One of the park's most striking features is its geology. The bright red Aztec sandstone formations, sculpted by millions of years of erosion, create a breathtaking landscape of towering cliffs, narrow canyons, and unique rock formations. Iconic landmarks include the Fire Wave, Arch Rock, and Elephant Rock, each offering picturesque views and fantastic photo opportunities.

Valley of Fire is also rich in ancient history, with numerous petroglyph sites dating back over 2,000 years. These rock carvings, created by the early Ancestral Puebloans, depict animals, humans, and abstract symbols, providing a fascinating glimpse into the region's prehistoric cultures. The Mouse's Tank and Atlatl Rock are popular sites where visitors can view these ancient artworks up close.

The park offers a variety of outdoor activities for visitors to enjoy. Hiking is a major draw, with several well-marked trails that cater to different skill levels. The White Domes Trail, a 1.1-mile loop, takes hikers through a colorful slot canyon and past scenic vistas, while the more challenging Fire Wave Trail leads to one of the park's most photographed rock formations.

Camping is another popular activity in Valley of Fire, with two main campgrounds offering both tent and RV sites. These campgrounds provide a serene setting to enjoy the desert's natural beauty and starlit skies. For those seeking more comfort, the park also has a visitor center with exhibits, a gift shop, and restrooms.

Wildlife enthusiasts will find the park teeming with desert species such as bighorn sheep, lizards, and a variety of birds. The spring and fall seasons are particularly pleasant for wildlife viewing, as temperatures are mild and animals are more active.

Overall, Valley of Fire State Park offers a unique and awe-inspiring desert landscape that attracts nature lovers, photographers, and outdoor enthusiasts. Its stunning scenery, rich history, and diverse recreational opportunities make it a must-visit destination for anyone exploring the Las Vegas area.

Mount Charleston

Mount Charleston, located just 35 miles northwest of Las Vegas, is a stunning alpine retreat that offers a refreshing contrast to the desert landscape of the Las Vegas Valley. Part of the Spring Mountains National Recreation Area, Mount Charleston is the highest peak in southern Nevada, rising to an elevation of 11,916 feet. Known for its cooler temperatures, lush forests, and diverse recreational opportunities, Mount Charleston is a popular destination for both locals and tourists seeking outdoor adventure and natural beauty.

The area surrounding Mount Charleston features a range of ecosystems, from desert scrub at lower elevations to bristlecone pine forests and alpine meadows higher up. This diversity supports a wide variety of plant and animal life, including mule deer, wild horses, and numerous bird species. The changing seasons bring different experiences, with wildflower blooms in the spring and vibrant foliage in the fall.

Hiking is one of the main attractions at Mount Charleston, with over 50 miles of trails catering to all skill levels. Popular hikes include the Mary Jane Falls Trail, a moderately challenging route that leads to a picturesque waterfall and cave, and the Cathedral Rock Trail, which offers panoramic views of the surrounding peaks and valleys. For those seeking a more strenuous adventure, the South Loop Trail provides a challenging ascent to the summit of Mount Charleston, rewarding hikers with breathtaking vistas and a sense of accomplishment.

In the winter, Mount Charleston transforms into a snowy wonderland, attracting visitors for skiing, snowboarding, and snowshoeing. The Lee Canyon Ski Resort offers a range of slopes for all skill levels, as well as lessons and equipment rentals. Sledding and tubing are also popular winter activities, making Mount Charleston a family-friendly destination year-round.

Camping is another favored activity, with several campgrounds and picnic areas available. These sites offer a peaceful setting to enjoy the mountain's natural beauty and provide a perfect base for exploring the trails and attractions. The Spring Mountains Visitor Gateway offers information, exhibits, and educational programs, helping visitors learn more about the area's natural and cultural history.

Overall, Mount Charleston provides a serene and scenic escape from the hustle and bustle of Las Vegas. Its diverse recreational opportunities, stunning landscapes, and cooler climate make it an ideal destination for outdoor enthusiasts and nature lovers.

Springs Preserve Botanical Garden

The Springs Preserve Botanical Garden, located just three miles from the Las Vegas Strip, is a lush oasis that showcases the beauty and diversity of desert plant life. Part of the larger Springs Preserve, a 180-acre cultural and historical site, the Botanical Garden is dedicated to the conservation, education, and appreciation of desert ecosystems. It offers visitors a tranquil retreat where they can explore a wide variety of plant species and learn about sustainable gardening practices.

The Botanical Garden spans over eight acres and features a diverse collection of plants from arid regions around the world. The garden is divided into themed sections, each highlighting different aspects of desert flora and landscaping. Visitors can stroll through the Cactus and Succulent Garden, which showcases an impressive array of cacti, agaves, and other succulents, including rare and endangered species. The Mojave Desert Garden highlights native plants of the region, demonstrating their adaptations to the harsh desert environment.

One of the key features of the Springs Preserve Botanical Garden is its emphasis on sustainable gardening and water conservation. The garden includes demonstration areas that illustrate techniques such as xeriscaping, rainwater harvesting, and the use of drought-tolerant plants. These exhibits provide practical information for homeowners and gardeners looking to create beautiful, water-efficient landscapes in arid climates.

The garden also features several scenic trails and pathways, allowing visitors to explore at their own pace. Informational signs and interactive displays provide insights into the plants and their ecological importance, enhancing the educational experience. Seasonal events and guided tours offer additional opportunities to learn about desert gardening and conservation.

In addition to its plant collections, the Botanical Garden is home to several art installations and sculptures that add to the visual appeal. The garden's design incorporates elements of beauty and functionality, creating a harmonious blend of art and nature.

The Springs Preserve Botanical Garden is part of the larger Springs Preserve complex, which includes museums, galleries, and historical exhibits. Visitors can explore the Origen Museum, which delves into the history and culture of the Las Vegas Valley, or the Nevada State Museum, which offers exhibits on the state's natural and cultural heritage.

Overall, the Springs Preserve Botanical Garden provides a serene and educational experience that highlights the beauty and resilience of desert plants. Its commitment to conservation and sustainability makes it a valuable resource for the community and a must-visit destination for anyone interested in the natural world.

Food and Dining

Iconic Las Vegas Foods

Las Vegas is a city known for its vibrant culinary scene, featuring a mix of high-end dining, international flavors, and classic American comfort foods. Some foods have become synonymous with the Las Vegas experience, offering visitors a taste of the city's unique gastronomic landscape. From extravagant buffets to shrimp cocktails and steak dinners, each iconic Las Vegas dish has its own story and renowned spots where you can savor the best versions.

Buffets

Las Vegas is famous for its extravagant buffets, which offer a vast array of dishes to suit every palate. These buffets are known for their abundance, variety, and high-quality ingredients, making them a quintessential part of the Las Vegas dining experience.

The concept of the Las Vegas buffet began in the 1940s with El Rancho Vegas, the city's first hotel-casino. The buffet was designed to keep gamblers inside the casino by offering a wide variety of food at a reasonable price.

Highlights:

- **Variety:** Buffets in Las Vegas offer everything from seafood and prime rib to sushi, international dishes, and decadent desserts.
- **Quality:** Many buffets source high-quality ingredients and feature live cooking stations where chefs prepare dishes to order.

Top Buffets in Las Vegas:
- **Bacchanal Buffet (Caesars Palace):** Known for its extensive selection and high-end offerings, including king crab legs, prime rib, and a wide variety of international cuisines.

- **Wicked Spoon (The Cosmopolitan):** Features individually plated dishes and a mix of traditional and contemporary flavors.
- **The Buffet at Wynn:** Offers a luxurious dining experience with over 120 dishes, including a notable selection of vegan and vegetarian options.

Shrimp Cocktail

The shrimp cocktail is another iconic Las Vegas dish, historically known for being a cheap and tasty treat enjoyed by visitors.

The shrimp cocktail became famous in Las Vegas in the 1950s at the Golden Gate Casino, where it was offered for just 50 cents. It quickly became a popular draw for tourists and locals alike.

Classic Preparation: The traditional shrimp cocktail consists of chilled, cooked shrimp served with a tangy cocktail sauce, often featuring a spicy kick from horseradish.

Presentation: Typically served in a glass with a wedge of lemon for garnish.

Top Places for Shrimp Cocktail in Las Vegas:

- **Golden Gate Casino:** The original home of the Las Vegas shrimp cocktail, where you can still enjoy this classic dish.
- **Du-Par's Restaurant and Bakery:** Located in the Golden Gate Hotel & Casino, offering a traditional shrimp cocktail that honors the city's culinary history.
- **Joe's Seafood, Prime Steak & Stone Crab:** Known for its fresh seafood, including a premium shrimp cocktail.

Steak

Las Vegas is renowned for its steakhouses, where visitors can indulge in premium cuts of beef prepared to perfection. The city's steakhouses range from classic to contemporary, each offering a unique dining experience.

The steakhouse culture in Las Vegas dates back to the mid-20th century, when the city began to attract high-rolling gamblers and celebrities, creating a demand for upscale dining establishments.

Highlights:

- **Quality Cuts:** Steakhouses in Las Vegas serve top-tier beef, including USDA Prime, Wagyu, and dry-aged steaks.
- **Luxurious Experience:** Many steakhouses offer elegant settings, exceptional service, and extensive wine lists.

Top Steakhouses in Las Vegas:

- **SW Steakhouse (Wynn):** Features premium cuts of beef and breathtaking views of the Lake of Dreams.
- **CUT by Wolfgang Puck (The Palazzo):** Known for its contemporary menu and high-quality steaks, including Japanese Wagyu.
- **Oscar's Steakhouse (Plaza Hotel):** Offers a classic Vegas experience with an old-school ambiance and delicious steaks.

Whether you're indulging in an opulent buffet, savoring a classic shrimp cocktail, or enjoying a luxurious steak dinner, Las Vegas' iconic foods offer a memorable culinary adventure. Each dish represents a piece of the city's rich and diverse food culture, making your dining experience in Las Vegas truly unique.

Fine Dining

Las Vegas is renowned for its world-class dining scene, offering exquisite culinary experiences that attract food enthusiasts from around the globe. The city's fine dining scene is characterized by its diversity, innovation, and the presence of numerous Michelin-starred restaurants.

Michelin-Starred Restaurants

Las Vegas boasts an impressive number of Michelin-starred restaurants, representing a wide array of cuisines and styles. These establishments are known for their meticulous attention to detail, exceptional service, and the use of the finest ingredients.

- **Joël Robuchon:** Located at the MGM Grand, this three Michelin-starred restaurant by the late Chef Joël Robuchon offers a luxurious dining experience. The elegant decor and perfectly executed French cuisine make it a must-visit for fine dining enthusiasts.

- **Restaurant Guy Savoy:** Situated in Caesars Palace, this two Michelin-starred restaurant by Chef Guy Savoy provides an intimate setting for savoring contemporary French dishes. Known for its artful presentations and impeccable service, it's a top choice for a special night out.
- **Twist by Pierre Gagnaire:** Found in the Waldorf Astoria, Twist offers an innovative menu that reflects Chef Pierre Gagnaire's avant-garde approach to French cuisine. The stunning views of the Strip add to the exceptional dining experience.

Internationally Inspired Fine Dining

Las Vegas' fine dining scene also includes a variety of internationally inspired restaurants that bring global flavors to the city.

- **é by José Andrés:** This exclusive, hidden gem inside Jaleo at The Cosmopolitan features an intimate dining experience with a multi-course tasting menu that highlights avant-garde Spanish cuisine.
- **Raku:** Known for its authentic Japanese robata grill, Raku in Chinatown offers a refined yet unpretentious dining experience. The restaurant is a favorite among locals and visiting chefs alike.
- **Wing Lei:** The first Chinese restaurant in the U.S. to earn a Michelin star, Wing Lei at the Wynn serves an exquisite menu of Cantonese, Shanghai, and Sichuan dishes in a luxurious setting.

Casual Eateries

Las Vegas' casual eateries offer a more relaxed dining experience without compromising on quality. From neighborhood favorites to trendy cafes, these establishments provide a diverse range of delicious and affordable options.

Casual eateries are often beloved by locals for their cozy ambiance and consistently good food.

- **Honey Salt:** This Summerlin spot is known for its farm-to-table approach and comforting dishes like the Biloxi Buttermilk Fried Chicken Sandwich and Brown Bag Baked Apple Pie.
- **Lotus of Siam:** Often hailed as one of the best Thai restaurants in America, this off-Strip gem offers a menu rich with Northern Thai flavors. The Khao Soi and Garlic Prawns are must-tries.
- **Tacos El Gordo:** Famous for its authentic Tijuana-style tacos, Tacos El Gordo on the Strip is a go-to for locals and tourists alike. The adobada (spicy pork) tacos are particularly popular.

Trendy Cafes and Diners

Las Vegas is also home to a plethora of trendy cafes and diners that serve up everything from classic American fare to innovative brunch dishes.

- **Eggslut:** Located inside The Cosmopolitan, Eggslut offers a menu centered around gourmet egg sandwiches. The Fairfax sandwich, with soft scrambled eggs and chives, is a crowd favorite.
- **The Peppermill:** An iconic Vegas diner known for its oversized portions and retro vibe, The Peppermill serves up classic American diner fare, including hearty breakfasts and famous fruit platters.
- **PublicUs:** This trendy downtown cafe is popular for its artisanal coffee and creative menu, which includes dishes like the Avocado Toast with a twist and the Breakfast Burrito.

Las Vegas' dining scene provides an array of options to suit every palate and occasion. Whether you're indulging in an opulent fine dining experience, savoring international flavors, or enjoying a casual meal at a beloved neighborhood spot, the city's culinary offerings are sure to leave a lasting impression.

Street Food and Food Trucks

Las Vegas' street food and food truck scene is vibrant and diverse, offering a quick and delicious way to sample a wide range of cuisines. From classic street eats to gourmet food trucks, these mobile eateries are an integral part of the city's culinary landscape.

Classic Street Food

Las Vegas' classic street food vendors have become iconic symbols of the city's fast-paced lifestyle. In addition to hot dogs, street carts in the city offer:

- **Pretzels:** Soft pretzels, often sold from carts on busy street corners, are a popular snack. These warm, salty treats are perfect for a quick bite on the go.
- **Tacos:** Mexican street food is a staple in Las Vegas. Tacos, whether from food trucks or street vendors, are beloved by both locals and tourists. Options range from traditional carne asada and al pastor to creative fusion varieties.

Gourmet Food Trucks

Las Vegas' food truck scene has exploded in recent years, with gourmet trucks offering inventive and high-quality dishes from around the world.

- **Fukuburger:** This food truck combines American and Japanese flavors, serving up delicious dishes like the Fuku Burger with all-beef patty, American cheese, and wasabi mayo, and the Tamago Burger with a fried egg.
- **Stripchezze:** Known for its gourmet grilled cheese sandwiches, Stripchezze offers creative takes on a classic comfort food. Favorites include the Mac N' Cheese Melt and the BBQ Pulled Pork Melt.
- **Dragon Grille:** Specializing in Asian fusion cuisine, Dragon Grille offers dishes like Korean BBQ beef tacos, garlic shrimp rice bowls, and crispy pork belly sliders.

In addition to individual food trucks, Las Vegas hosts several pop-up markets where multiple vendors gather to offer a variety of street food options.

- **Fergusons Downtown:** This revitalized space in downtown Las Vegas hosts food trucks and pop-up events, offering a diverse range of street food from local vendors. It's a great spot to find unique and delicious eats in a lively atmosphere.
- **First Friday:** Held on the first Friday of each month, this arts and culture festival in the Arts District features a variety of food trucks and street vendors. Visitors can enjoy an eclectic mix of food while exploring local art and live music.

Ethnic Cuisine

Las Vegas is a melting pot of cultures, and its diverse neighborhoods offer a rich tapestry of ethnic cuisines. Chinatown, the Italian American Club, and the Hispanic community in East Las Vegas are some of the most vibrant areas where visitors can indulge in authentic and delicious foods from around the world.

Chinatown

Chinatown in Las Vegas is one of the city's most dynamic culinary hubs, established by Asian immigrants in the late 20th century. Located along Spring Mountain Road, this area is bustling with markets, bakeries, and restaurants showcasing a wide array of authentic Asian cuisine.

Highlights:

- **Dim Sum:** Traditional Cantonese dim sum is a popular choice, with restaurants like **KJ Dim Sum & Seafood** and **Ping Pang Pong** offering a variety of dumplings, buns, and other delicacies served from rolling carts.

- **Sichuan Cuisine:** For spicy Sichuan dishes, **Chengdu Taste** is a go-to spot, known for its bold flavors and mouth-numbing spices.
- **Japanese Cuisine: Raku** is celebrated for its authentic Japanese robata grill, offering refined yet unpretentious dishes like grilled skewers and agedashi tofu.
- **Street Markets:** Chinatown's street markets are filled with fresh produce, seafood, and exotic ingredients, providing a glimpse into the neighborhood's rich culinary traditions.

East Las Vegas Hispanic Community

East Las Vegas is home to a vibrant Hispanic community, offering a plethora of authentic Mexican and Latin American culinary experiences. From street food to sit-down restaurants, this area is rich in flavor and cultural heritage.

Highlights:

- **Tacos: Tacos El Gordo** is famous for its authentic Tijuana-style tacos, with offerings like adobada (spicy pork), carne asada, and lengua (beef tongue).
- **Street Vendors:** The streets of East Las Vegas are dotted with vendors selling everything from elote (Mexican street corn) to churros, providing a true taste of Latin American street food culture.
- **Latin American Cuisine:** Restaurants like **Mariscos Playa Escondida** serve a variety of dishes from across Latin America, including ceviche, pupusas, and arepas.

Food Markets

Las Vegas is renowned for its diverse culinary landscape, and its food markets are some of the best places to experience this gastronomic variety. Among these, the Downtown Container Park and the Las Vegas Farmers Market stand out as must-visit destinations for food lovers seeking a wide array of flavors and culinary delights.

Downtown Container Park

Located in the Fremont East District, the Downtown Container Park is a unique open-air shopping and dining center constructed from repurposed shipping containers. It offers a variety of food options in a lively and family-friendly environment.

Highlights:

- **Diverse Food Options:** The park features an eclectic mix of eateries, from gourmet burgers at **Big Ern's BBQ** to health-conscious fare at **Simply Pure**.
- **Live Entertainment:** Visitors can enjoy live music and performances while sampling a range of delicious foods.
- **Artisan Shops:** In addition to food, the Container Park offers boutique shops and art galleries, making it a great spot for a leisurely outing.

Las Vegas Farmers Market

The Las Vegas Farmers Market operates at various locations throughout the city, offering fresh, locally sourced produce and a variety of artisanal foods.

Highlights:

- **Fresh Produce:** Visitors can purchase fresh fruits, vegetables, and herbs from local farmers.
- **Artisan Foods:** The market features vendors selling homemade jams, baked goods, and specialty items like honey and artisanal cheeses.
- **Food Trucks:** Many markets include food trucks offering a range of cuisines, from Mexican street food to gourmet sandwiches.

Both the Downtown Container Park and the Las Vegas Farmers Market offer unique and memorable culinary experiences, showcasing the best of Las Vegas' vibrant food scene. Whether you're exploring the eclectic offerings at the Container Park or enjoying the fresh, local flavors at the Farmers Market, these food markets are essential destinations for any food enthusiast visiting the city.

Made in United States
Troutdale, OR
03/19/2025

29892782R00056